The Way of Love

READINGS FOR A MEANINGFUL LIFE

Other titles in this series:

The Way of Gratitude: Readings for a Joyful Life

The Way of Kindness: Readings for a Graceful Life

The Way of Forgiveness: Readings for a Peaceful Life

The Way of Suffering: Readings for an Enlightened Life

The Way of Peace: Readings for a Harmonious Life

The Way of Love

Readings for a Meaningful Life

Michael Leach, Doris Goodnough,
Maria Angelini, editors

ORBIS BOOKS
Maryknoll, New York 10545

Founded in 1970, Orbis Books endeavors to publish works that enlighten the mind, nourish the spirit, and challenge the conscience. The publishing arm of the Maryknoll Fathers and Brothers, Orbis seeks to explore the global dimensions of the Christian faith and mission, to invite dialogue with diverse cultures and religious traditions, and to serve the cause of reconciliation and peace. The books published reflect the views of their authors and do not represent the official position of the Maryknoll Society. To learn more about Orbis Books, please visit our website at www.orbisbooks.com.

Library of Congress Cataloging-in-Publication Data

Names: Leach, Michael, editor. | Goodnough, Doris, editor. | Angelini, Maria, editor.

Title: The way of love : readings for a meaningful life / Michael Leach, Doris Goodnough, Maria Angelini.

Description: Maryknoll : Orbis Books, 2022. | Series: The way | Includes bibliographical references and index.

Identifiers: LCCN 2021050710 | ISBN 9781626984653 (trade paperback)

Subjects: LCSH: Love—Religious aspects—Christianity—Literary collections. | Love—Religious aspects—Literary collections.

Classification: LCC BV4639 .W34 2022 | DDC 231/.6—dc23/eng/20211130

LC record available at https://lccn.loc.gov/2021050710

Love never fails.

—John 14:27

Contents

Introduction
page 1

PART ONE
LOVE

1
Fall in Love
JOSEPH WHELAN
page 7

2
Love Is the Love
of Being Loving
MICHAEL LEACH
page 8

3
All Things Work Together for Good
to Those Who Love Being Loving
THOMAS HORA
page 12

THE WAY OF LOVE

4

Unconditional Love

HAROLD W. BECKER

page 14

Love Notes

ELISABETH KÜBLER-ROSS, RAM DASS,
WILLIAM SHAKESPEARE, DONNA GODDARD

page 15

5

When Love Beckons, Follow

KAHLIL GIBRAN

page 17

6

*The Intuitive Knowledge
of the Heart*

MARIANNE WILLIAMSON

page 20

7

We Are Love with Skin On

ANNE LAMOTT

page 22

Contents

8

I Know Who She Is
UNKNOWN
page 25

Love Notes
FORREST GUMP (TOM HANKS),
DESMOND TUTU, DOROTHY DAY,
MELVIN UDALL (JACK NICHOLSON)
page 26

9

The Gift of Love
I CORINTHIANS 13: I–13
page 28

10

The Qualities of Love
ANTHONY DE MELLO
page 30

11

You Will Truly Serve Only What You Love
STEPHEN COLBERT
page 34

THE WAY OF LOVE

12

*Justice Is What Love
Looks Like In Public*
PHILIP WALSH
page 37

13

Love and the Purpose of Life
MOTHER TERESA
page 40

Love Notes
ERICH FROMM, JORDAN PETERSON
VICTOR FRANKL, MAYA ANGELOU
page 43

14

The Daring Adventure of Love
ILIA DELIO
page 45

15

Love Is for Living
CARLO CARRETTO
page 47

Contents

16

Love Is Mysterious
JACK KORNFIELD
page 49

17

Love Sails Me around the House
THOMAS MERTON
page 51

Love Notes
JAMES BALDWIN, ZORA NEALE HURSTON,
FYODOR DOSTOEVSKY, CHARLES M. SCHULZ
page 53

18

What Is This Thing Called Love?
MATTHEW FOX
page 55

19

This Is Love, Become Love, Be That One
ECKHART TOLLE, MEISTER ECKHART,
AND SHERI BESSI-ECKERT
page 60

THE WAY OF LOVE

20

The Power of Love
(or Imagine a World Where Love Is the Way)
BISHOP MICHAEL CURRY

page 62

PART TWO
LOVE OF GOD

21

May We Remember That God Is the Only Love
DONNA GODDARD

page 67

22

What Do I Love When I Love God
ST. AUGUSTINE

page 68

23

God's Signature
ERNESTO CARDENAL

page 69

24

Start with Loving a Stone
RICHARD ROHR

page 70

Contents

25

God Is the Ocean in Which We All Swim
PATRICK T. REARDON
page 72

26

Our Love Flows from the Love of God
SØREN KIERKEGAARD
page 76

Love Notes
1 JOHN 4:16, ACTS 17:28, GENESIS 1:26, GENESIS 1:31
FYODOR DOSTOEVSKY, COLOSSIANS 3:14
page 78

27

We Love Because He First Loved Us
ROBERT ELLSBERG
page 80

28

I Am Sustained by the Love of God
A COURSE IN MIRACLES
page 82

29

God Is a Mother, Too
VICKIE LEACH
page 84

The Way of Love

30

God Is My Everything
Thea Bowman
page 87

Love Notes
Meister Eckhart, 1 Samuel 16:7,
Gerard Manley Hopkins, Óscar Romero
Genesis 16:13
page 88

31

*Quick, Open the Door,
It's God Coming to Love Us!*
Madeleine Delbrêl
page 90

32

I Love You for Sentimental Reasons
Marion Amberg
page 93

33

God
Brian Doyle
page 97

Contents

34

*God Owns a Convenience Store
in British Columbia—
Who Knew?*
GAE RUSK
page 99

Love Notes
SUE MONK KIDD, MAYA ANGELOU, ANNE LAMOTT,
THOMAS HORA, VINCENT DE PAUL
page 103

35

The Parable of the Prodigal Son
LUKE 15:11–32
page 106

36

This Tremendous Lover
DOM EUGENE BOYLAN
page 108

37

Don't Give Up on God, or Yourself
JOSEPHINE ROBERTSON
page 111

THE WAY OF LOVE

38

That We May Love as You Love!
UNKNOWN
page 114

39

"I Am Wherever There Is Love"
JOY SCRIVENER
page 115

Love Notes
MEISTER ECKHART, ST. AUGUSTINE
page 118

PART THREE
LOVE OF NEIGHBOR

40

The Parable of the Good Samaritan
LUKE 10:25–37
page 121

41

Who Is My Neighbor?
FREDERIC BUECHNER
page 123

Contents

42

Love Your Neighbor
CYNTHIA BOURGEAULT
page 124

43

Love Whatever Arises
MATT KAHN
page 126

44

Love from Neighbors on the Margins
EDWINA GATELEY
page 128

45

When You Thought I Wasn't Looking
MARY RITA SCHILKE SILL
page 130

46

Loving-Kindness:
Blessing Your Corner
of the World with Love
VICTOR PARACHIN
page 132

THE WAY OF LOVE

Love Notes
1 JOHN 4:7-8, ILIA DELIO,
C. S. LEWIS, KURT VONNEGUT JR.,
NICOLAS CHAMFORT
page 136

47
Love Your Enemies
MATTHEW AND LUKE
page 138

48
We Love Each Other
That's Enough
RAM DASS AND PAUL GORMAN
page 140

49
Save Your Best for Someone Else
DONNA ASHWORTH
page 143

50
Love at Its Best
JOHN LEWIS
page 145

Contents

Love Notes
Glenn Beck,
Acts 4:32–35, Michael Leach
page 146

51
Why Are You Here?
Vincent P. Cole
page 148

52
Stand Up for the Stupid and Crazy
Walt Whitman
page 149

53
Love Deeply
Henri J. M. Nouwen
page 150

Love Notes
Dorothy Day, Donna Goddard,
Søren Kierkegaard,
Mr. Rogers
page 152

THE WAY OF LOVE

54

A Piece of Light
JOYCE RUPP
page 154

55

Tend to What Repulses You
PAULINE HOVEY
page 156

56

Don't Look Away
BRENÉ BROWN
page 161

57

Having Lunch with God
JOSEPH HEALEY
page 162

58

Bishop Morrie Says
It's Not about the Soup
MICHAEL LEACH
page 164

Contents

59

It All Tastes Like Love
FRAN ROSSI SZPYLCZYN
page 169

60

A Marriage, an Elegy
WENDELL BERRY
page 173

Love Notes
HENRI J. M. NOUWEN, GERALD MAY
L. R. KNOST, ROBIN WILLIAMS
page 174

61

Loving the Christ in Others
THOMAS MERTON
page 176

62

Christ, Let Me See You in Others
DAVID ADAM
page 178

63

Christ and Cerebral Palsy
MICHAEL LEACH
page 179

Love Notes

MOTHER TERESA, I CORINTHIANS 12:12
I CORINTHIANS 12:26,
PIERRE TEILHARD DE CHARDIN, ROBERT ADAMS
page 183

64

Christ in the Subway
CARYLL HOUSELANDER
page 185

65

God's Disguise
MOTHER TERESA
page 187

66

*Remember,
There Is the Face of Christ*
ÓSCAR ROMERO
page 188

Contents

67

Christ in the Poor
JIM FOREST
page 189

68

We're All God's Children
DENNIS MOORMAN
page 190

Love Notes
A COURSE IN MIRACLES,
JOHN 14:20, RUMI
page 192

Sources and Acknowledgments
page 195

Contributors
page 203

Nor height, nor depth, nor anything else in all creation, will be able to separate us from the love of God in Christ Jesus our Lord.

—ROMANS 8:39

Introduction

Everyone has a philosophy of life. For Terry Malloy (Marlon Brando) in the 1954 movie *On the Waterfront*, it was "Do it to him before he does it to you." Terry falls in love with a convent girl, Edie (Eva Marie Saint), who asks him, "Shouldn't everybody care about everybody else?" He calls her a fruitcake.

"I mean," says Edie, "isn't everybody *a part* of everybody else?" This is her philosophy of life.

Later Terry crosses paths with Fr. Barry (Karl Malden), whose parish is the rough waterfront of New Jersey, and he too has a philosophy of life. When the mob murders a longshoreman, Fr. Barry stands over the corpse in the hole and preaches to the other longshoremen, one of whom says he should go back to his church:

> "Boys, this is my church! And if you don't think Christ is down here on the waterfront, you've got another think coming! Every morning when the hiring boss blows his whistle, Jesus stands alongside you in the shape-up. He sees why some of you get picked and some of you get passed over. He sees the family men worrying about getting the rent

and getting food in the house for the wife and the kids. . . . Every fellow down here is your brother in Christ! . . . He's kneeling right here beside Dugan. And he's saying with all of you, if you do it to the least of mine, you do it to me!"

The words pierce Terry Malloy's heart like the spear that ran through Jesus's side. He starts to see what Edie sees: we are part of one another. His conscience stirs. "Conscience," he complains to Fr. Barry later, "that stuff can drive you nuts!" It drives him instead into Edie's arms and to a new philosophy of life. At the end of the movie Terry carries his hook over his shoulder like a cross and stands up for love, for God, for Edie, and for his neighbors.

On the Waterfront. What a great movie! If you watch it you don't have to read this book.

It's OK if you do both though.

Our point is, everyone has a philosophy of life. And, like love, as the Andrew Lloyd Weber song goes, "It changes everything, how we live and how we die."

Our philosophy in *The Way of Love* is much like Edie's and Fr. Barry's and later Terry's, expressed in a multitude of ways by more than a hundred writers. You can read it from beginning to end or in chunks if you wish and, we hope, find something new or something you forgot that will give you a bit of inspiration or encouragement or assurance. Just as good, you can pick it up every now and then and turn to any old page and, we hope, find something that will help make your day.

The book is divided into three parts, each with a basic theme. The theme is like a hub in a bicycle wheel with enough spokes spreading out to keep you moving forward into practical and sometimes surprising places.

Part One, "Love," does what most books on the subject don't do. It gives a definition of love. Most books describe love, and make distinctions like *eros* and *agape,* without ever saying in a simple sentence what love is. We like the definition given by Dr. Thomas Hora, a psychiatrist and spiritual teacher: "Love, which comes from God, is the love of being loving. When we fall in love with the love of being loving—*unconditional spiritual benevolence*—Love, or God, reveals itself through us and all things work together for good."

Part Two then is "Love of God." Its basic premise is that God is the only love there is. We love because God loves us first. God is not a person outside us but Love and Wisdom within us and all around us. God is all powerful, everywhere active Good. To love loving what is good and beautiful and merciful is to love God. When we are filled with unconditional benevolence we overflow with God.

Part Three, "Love of Neighbor," is about that overflow. It helps us know what Edie knew—everybody is a part of everybody—and what Fr. Barry preached—we are all manifestations of one God, so what we do to our neighbor we do to the Christ in ourselves. Just as a wave can never be separated from the sea or from the other waves, we can never be separated from Christ or from one another. The wave is in the ocean, and the ocean is in the wave. We are in God, and God is in us. This is the basis for loving our neighbor as ourself. The implications are mind-boggling.

The Way of Love is the sixth book in a series that includes *The Way of Kindness*, *The Way of Gratitude*, *The Way of Forgiveness*, *The Way of Suffering*, and *The Way of Peace*. Just as we have endeavored to make the three parts of this book, and all the entries in each part, lead one into another, we have tried to make each book in the series an integral aspect of all the other books. Our philosophy is not only that everybody is a part of everybody else, but that everything is a part of everything. Everything on the waterfront is *one*.

With all our love,

MICHAEL LEACH
DORIS GOODNOUGH
MARIA ANGELINI

PART ONE

LOVE

Love is the love of being loving
—THOMAS HORA

Fall in Love

Joseph Whelan

Nothing is more practical than
finding God, than
falling in Love
in a quite absolute, final way.
What you are in love with,
what seizes your imagination, will affect
    everything.
It will decide
what will get you out of bed in the
    morning,
what you do with your evenings,
how you spend your weekends,
what you read, whom you know,
what breaks your heart,
and what amazes you with joy and
    gratitude.
Fall in Love, stay in love,
and it will decide everything.

Love Is the Love of Being Loving

Michael Leach

"Loretta, I love you. Not like they told you love is, and I didn't know this either, but love don't make things nice—it ruins everything. It breaks your heart. It makes things a mess. We aren't here to make things perfect. The snowflakes are perfect. The stars are perfect. Not us. Not us! We are here to ruin ourselves and to break our hearts and love the wrong people and die." . . .
"I'm in love with you."

—RONNY (NICOLAS CAGE)
IN *MOONSTRUCK*

"Snap out of it!"

—LORETTA (CHER)

8

Like Ronny and Loretta, first we fall in love. That's the exciting part. Then we learn to love. That's the hard part. Finally, we simply love being loving. And that, by far, is the best part.

My favorite movie about love is *Fargo*. That's the one where Steve Buscemi gets stuffed into a wood chipper. But it's really about Marge Gunderson (Frances McDormand), a pregnant sheriff, and her husband, Norm (John Carroll Lynch), who gets out of bed to make her a hot breakfast when she's called to a crime scene at 3 a.m. He goes out and warms up her car because it's below zero and snowing. The best scene comes at the end when Marge and Norm are lying in bed and he confesses that his painting of a mallard for a new stamp came in second place.

"Oh, that's terrific," Marge says.

"It's just a 3-cent stamp."

"It's terrific."

"Haupman's blue-winged teal got the 29-cent. People don't much use the 3-cent."

"Oh, for Pete's sake, of course they do! Whenever they raise the postage, people need the little stamps."

"Yah?"

"When they're stuck with a bunch of the old ones."

"Yah, I guess."

"It's terrific. I'm so proud of you, Norm. . . . Heck, Norm, you know we're doing pretty good."

Norm caresses Marge's pregnant belly. "I love you, Margie."

"I love you, Norm."

"Two more months," he says.

"Two more months."

That's all there is. That's all there needs to be. We don't need the moon to hit our eye like a big pizza pie to know *amore*. Marge and Norm know that love is not excitement but the steadfast love of being loving.

Actors Ruby Dee and Ossie Davis, married for 56 years, knew about that kind of love. In her autobiography Ruby wrote about the arrangement they made for after their deaths: "A special urn, large enough and comfortable enough to hold both our ashes. Whoever goes first will wait inside for the other. When we are reunited at last, we want the family to say good-bye and seal the urn forever. Then on the side, in letters not too bold—but not too modest either—we want the following inscription: RUBY AND OSSIE—IN THIS THING TOGETHER."

We can begin to love being loving whether we're in love or not, in a relationship or not, right here on the spot where we're standing. We are all Ruby and Ossie. We are all in this thing together. We are all literally "in Love" (Acts 17:28), and our purpose in life is to see it and be it no matter our age or state of life. Real love has no beginning, object, or end.

Psychiatrist Thomas Hora defines this love for us: "The love of being loving is the desire to manifest or reflect the goodness of God unconditionally and non-personally." God is all powerful, all everywhere Love-being-loving. We are not here to ruin ourselves and break our hearts and love the wrong people and die, but to love the way God loves

(John 13:34), without desire for reward or regard for person. We are all Ronny and Loretta and Marge and Norm too: likenesses of Love and in this thing called Love as one, like ashes in an urn.

Falling in love is such fun, and such misery. Learning to love—snapping out of it—is so hard. The love of being loving—being Godlike—is the best part. And the beautiful part is that we can start that part right now.

All Things Work Together for Good to Those Who Love Being Loving

Thomas Hora

Every one of us needs to learn to love the way God loves. After all, we are manifestations of Love-Intelligence, which is God. We are the image and likeness of God. We are all capable of manifesting spiritual love.

Spiritual love, derived from Love-Intelligence, is non-conditional, nonpersonal (or transpersonal) benevolence. It is the love of being loving, with no strings attached, just for the sake of being what God wants us to be. When we are loving in this sense, we are manifesting God's love, or we may say, God's love is expressing itself through us.

What do we mean by nonpersonal or transpersonal love? It is love that gives itself. We do not personally give love, we become instruments of this love. We do not produce love, we allow love to express itself through us. That is prayer in action. How do we do that? How do we reach that point where this can happen? By being *interested* in it. We can say: To be enlightened is easy, it's just difficult to be interested in it. The word "interest" consists of the word *inter-esse*, which means to be between, that is, to be involved. To be interested in something means to be mentally involved with it.

Enlightened human love is nonconditional. It says, "I love you just the way you are; I make no conditions; you don't have to like spinach, and you don't have to wear your hair in a certain way." Conditional love is more harmful than neglect. If we are neglected, at least we are free to make our own mistakes and learn from them. But if we are loved conditionally, it enslaves us. Conditional love is disabling; nonconditional love is empowering.

~~~

There is a universal benevolence enveloping us all.

Unconditional Love

Harold W. Becker

The greatest power known to man is that of unconditional love. Through the ages, mystics, sages, singers, and poets have all expressed the ballad and call to love. As humans, we have searched endlessly for the experience of love through the outer senses. Great nations have come and gone under the guise of love for their people. Religions have flourished and perished while claiming the true path to love. We, the people of this planet, may have missed the simplicity of unconditional love. . . .

Simply stated, unconditional love is an unlimited way of being. We are without any limit to our thoughts and feelings in life and can create any reality we choose to focus our attention upon. There are infinite imaginative possibilities when we allow the freedom to go beyond our perceived limits. If we can dream it, we can build it. Life, through unconditional love, is a wondrous adventure that excites the very core of our being and lights our path with delight.

Love Notes

*The ultimate lesson all of us have
to learn is unconditional love, which
includes not only others but ourselves
as well.*

—ELISABETH KÜBLER-ROSS

*Unconditional love really exists in each
of us. It is part of our deep inner being.
It is not so much an active emotion as
a state of being. It's not "I love you"
for this or that reason, not "I love you
if you love me." It's love for no reason,
love without an object.*

—RAM DASS

*Love is not love
Which alters when it alteration finds,
Or bends with the remover to remove:
O no! it is an ever-fixed mark*

*That looks on tempests and is never
shaken.*

—WILLIAM SHAKESPEARE, *SONNET 116*

*To understand the love of being loving
radically changes us. People, in and of
themselves, cannot give us happiness.
Activities, in an of themselves, cannot
give us happiness. One becomes a loving presence, a center for Divine grace.
. . . Love is inclusive of everyone and
has no ulterior motive. . . . Do not be
afraid of love or the course it will take.
There is no certainty in life. Choose
love first and choose love last and it
will give you more than you ever give it.*

—DONNA GODDARD

When Love Beckons, Follow

Kahlil Gibran

When love beckons to you, follow him,
Though his ways are hard and steep.
And when his wings enfold you yield to him,
Though the sword hidden among his pinions may wound
    you.
And when he speaks to you believe in him,
Though his voice may shatter your dreams
as the north wind lays waste the garden.

For even as love crowns you so shall he crucify you. Even
    as he is for your growth so is he for your pruning.
Even as he ascends to your height and caresses your tender-
    est branches that quiver in the sun,
So shall he descend to your roots and shake them in their
    clinging to the earth.
Like sheaves of corn he gathers you unto himself.
He threshes you to make you naked.
He sifts you to free you from your husks.

He grinds you to whiteness.

He kneads you until you are pliant;

And then he assigns you to his sacred fire, that you may
become sacred bread for God's sacred feast.

All these things shall love do unto you that you may know
the secrets of your heart, and in that knowledge become
a fragment of Life's heart.

But if in your fear you would seek only love's peace and
love's pleasure,

Then it is better for you that you cover your nakedness and
pass out of love's threshing-floor,

Into the seasonless world where you shall laugh, but not
all of your laughter, and weep, but not all of your tears.

Love gives naught but itself and takes naught but from itself.

Love possesses not nor would it be possessed;

For love is sufficient unto love.

When you love you should not say, "God is in my heart,"
but rather, "I am in the heart of God."

And think not you can direct the course of love, for love, if
it finds you worthy, directs your course.

Love has no other desire but to fulfill itself.

But if you love and must needs have desires, let these be
your desires:

To melt and be like a running brook that sings its melody
to the night.

To know the pain of too much tenderness.
To be wounded by your own understanding of love;
And to bleed willingly and joyfully.

To wake at dawn with a winged heart and give thanks for
    another day of loving;
To rest at the noon hour and meditate love's ecstasy;
To return home at eventide with gratitude;
And then to sleep with a prayer for the beloved in your
    heart and a song of praise upon your lips.

The Intuitive Knowledge of the Heart

Marianne Williamson

Love isn't seen with the physical eyes or heard with the physical ears. The physical senses can't perceive it; it's perceived through another kind of vision. Metaphysicians call it the Third Eye, esoteric Christians call it the vision of the Holy Spirit, and others call it the Higher Self. Regardless of what it's called, love requires a different kind of "seeing" than we're used to—a different kind of knowing or thinking. Love is the intuitive knowledge of our hearts. It's a "world beyond" that we all secretly long for. An ancient memory of this love haunts all of us all the time, and beckons us to return.

Love isn't material. It's energy. It's the feeling in a room, a situation, a person. Money can't buy it. Sex doesn't guarantee it. It has nothing at all to do with the physical world, but it can be expressed nonetheless. We experience it as kindness, giving, mercy, compassion, peace, joy, acceptance, nonjudgment, joining, and intimacy.

><

> *It is only with the heart that one can*
> *see rightly. What is essential is invisible*
> *to the eye.*
> —ANTOINE DE SAINT-EXUPÉRY,
> *THE LITTLE PRINCE*

We Are Love with Skin On

Anne Lamott

It's not every day a girl turns 67. I never thought I'd see 18, and then 21, and then 30, and then 50! Half a century old. 17 years ago. And now here I am on Medicare, married two years ago to the coolest guy, with feet that hurt almost all the time, a mind that scares me with its increasing forgetfulness and snags, and a heart so filled with love some days that I feel like a moony teenager and probably should not be behind the wheel.

Other days, not so much.

It's frustrating to lose cognitive function, and for everything to ache the day after a hike. I take some medicine at night but ten minutes later, I can't be positive if I took it or not, and I have to compensate in a dozen ways for my constant distraction. I got a car five years ago designed for people who probably should not be driving. It has Keebler elves hidden behind the dashboard that beep when I am about to hit another car, or when the car in front of me has moved. The elves wipe at their foreheads at each near miss.

This is SO not who I am. You've got to believe me. I was the smartest girl in my algebra class junior year. I was a tennis champ. Now when I get out of bed in the morning, I limp around like Walter Brennan, and then I limp around off and on all day trying to remember what I am limping around looking for. There's a story in the new book about accidentally taking the dog's medicine, which was banned for humans by the FDA. I called the vet and said, "Oh, I'm sure you get this all the time." She said, "No, not really."

Yet this might be the happiest I've ever been. The original title of *Dusk Night Dawn* was *The Third Third*, about the great blessings of being older—the self-forgiveness, the grace of myopia, of not seeing everyone's flaws so clearly, the pleasures of a much quieter life, of slower and more attentive walks. But more than anything, the great blessing, the reason for my deep faith in life and God, is the minuet of old friendships.

As John Merrick, the Elephant Man said, "My life is full because I know that I am loved." That is exactly and 100% my truth. I learned in the last third of my life that love is all there is, that we are Love with skin on, that Blake was right when he wrote that we are here to learn to endure the beams of love. Love can be hard. We're good at hard.

I wrote in the new book, "Love is gentle if sometimes amused warmth for annoying and deeply disappointing people, especially ourselves. Love is someone who will draw near when you cry. Love plops in front of the TV with a bowl of popcorn and you. Love plops but love also flies. Love reveals the beauty of sketchy people like us to ourselves. Love holds up the sacred mirror. Love builds rickety greenhouses for our wilder seeds to grow. Love can be reckless (Jesus is good at this), or meek as my dog, or carry a briefcase. Love is the old man in the park teaching little kids to play the violin; much time spent tuning, the children hearing their way into the key he is playing. Love tiptoes and love lumbers like an elephant; it naps on top of your chest like a cat. It gooses you, snickers, smooths your hair. Love is being with a person wherever they are, however they are acting. Ugh. (A lot of things seem to come more easily to God.)

My life is full and I am grateful to the point of tears on my 67th birthday because I know I am loved. I just wanted to share that with you.

8

I Know Who She Is

Unknown

He is 85 and insists on taking his wife's hand everywhere they go. When I asked him why his wife kept looking away, he responded, "Because she has Alzheimer's."

I then asked him, "Will your wife worry if you let her go?"

He then replied, "She doesn't remember anything, she doesn't know who I am anymore, she hasn't recognized me for years."

Surprised, I said, "And you have continued to guide her every single day even though she doesn't recognize you?"

The elderly man smiled and looked into my eyes and said, "She may not know who I am, but I know who she is, and she is the love of my life."

A friend knows the song in my heart and sings it to me when my memory fails.

Love Notes

I may not be smart, but I know what love is.

—Forrest Gump (Tom Hanks)

It's like when you sit in front of a fire in winter—you are just there in front of the fire. You don't have to be smart or anything. The fire warms you.

—Desmond Tutu

Love and ever more love is the only solution to every problem that comes up. If we love each other enough, we will bear with each other's faults and burdens. If we love enough, we are going to light a fire in the hearts of others. And it is love that will burn out the sins and hatreds that sadden us. It is

Love Notes

*love that will make us want to do great
things for each other. No sacrifice and
no suffering will then seem too much.*

—DOROTHY DAY

You make me want to be a better man.

—MELVIN UDALL (JACK NICHOLSON)

9

The Gift of Love

1 Corinthians 13:1–13

If I speak with the tongues of mankind and of angels, but do not have love, I have become a noisy gong or a clanging cymbal. If I have the gift of prophecy and know all mysteries and all knowledge, and if I have all faith so as to remove mountains, but do not have love, I am nothing. And if I give away all my possessions to charity, and if I surrender my body so that I may glory, but do not have love, it does me no good.

Love is patient, love is kind, it is not jealous; love does not brag, it is not arrogant. It does not act disgracefully, it does not seek its own benefit; it is not provoked, does not keep an account of a wrong suffered, it does not rejoice in unrighteousness, but rejoices with the truth; it keeps every confidence, it believes all things, hopes all things, endures all things.

Love never fails; but if there are gifts of prophecy, they will be done away with; if there are tongues, they will cease; if there is knowledge, it will be done away with. For we know in part and prophesy in part; but when the perfect comes, the partial will be done away with. When I was a child, I used to speak like a child, think like a child, reason like a child; when I became a man, I did away with childish things. For now we see in a mirror dimly, but then face to face; now I know in part, but then I will know fully, just as I also have been fully known. But now faith, hope, and love remain, these three; but the greatest of these is love.

10

The Qualities of Love

Anthony de Mello

*This is my commandment, that you
love one another as I have loved you.*

—JOHN 15:12

What is love? Take a look at a rose. Is it possible for the
rose to say, "I shall offer my fragrance to good people and
withhold it from bad people?" Or can you imagine a lamp
that withholds its rays from a wicked person who seeks to
walk in its light? It could only do that by ceasing to be a
lamp. And observe how helplessly and indiscriminately a
tree gives its shade to everyone, good and bad, young and
old, high and low; to animals and humans and every living
creature—even to the one who seeks to cut it down. So
this is the first quality of love: its indiscriminate character.
That is why we are exhorted to be like God, "who makes
his sun to shine on good and bad alike and makes his rain to
fall on saints and sinners alike; so you must be all goodness
as your heavenly Father is all goodness." Contemplate in

astonishment the sheer goodness of the rose, the lamp, the tree, for there you have an image of what love is all about.

How does one attain this quality of love? Any thing you do will only make it forced, cultivated and therefore phony, for love cannot be forced. There is nothing you can do. But there is something you can drop. Observe the marvelous change that comes over you the moment you stop seeing people as good and bad, as saints and sinners, and begin to see them as unaware and ignorant. You must drop your false belief that people can sin in awareness. No one can sin in the light of awareness. Sin occurs, not, as we mistakenly think, in malice, but in ignorance. "Father, forgive them for they do not know what they are doing." To see this is to acquire the indiscriminate quality one so admires in the rose, the lamp and the tree.

And here is a second quality of love—its gratuitousness. Like the tree, the rose, the lamp, it gives and asks for nothing in return. How we despise the man whose choice of his wife is determined not by any quality she may have but by the amount of money she will bring as dowry. Such a man, we rightly say, loves not the woman but the financial benefit she brings him. But is your own love any different when you seek the company of those who bring you emotional gratification and avoid those who don't; when you are positively disposed toward people who give you what you want and live up to your expectations and are negative or indifferent toward those who don't? Here too there is only one thing that you need do to acquire this quality of gratuitousness that characterizes love. You can open your eyes and see. Just seeing, just exposing your so-called love for what it really is, a camouflage for selfishness and greed, is a major step toward arriving at this second quality of love.

The third quality of love is its unself-consciousness. Love so enjoys the loving that it is blissfully unaware of itself. The way the lamp is busy shining with no thought of whether it is benefiting others or not. The way a rose gives out its fragrance simply because there is nothing else it can do, whether there is someone to enjoy the fragrance or not. The way the tree offers its shade. The light, the fragrance and the shade are not produced at the approach of persons and turned off when there is no one there. These things, like love, exist independently of persons. Love simply is, it has no object. They simply are, regardless of whether someone will benefit from them or not. So they have no consciousness of any merit or of doing good. Their left hand has no consciousness of what their right hand does. "Lord, when did we see you hungry or thirsty and help you?"

The final quality of love is its freedom. The moment coercion or control or conflict enters, love dies. Think how the rose, the tree, the lamp leave you completely free. The tree will make no effort to drag you into its shade if you are in danger of a sunstroke. The lamp will not force its light on you lest you stumble in the dark. Think for a while of all the coercion and control that you submit to on the part of others when you so anxiously live up to their expectations in order to buy their love and approval or because you fear you will lose them. Each time you submit to this control and this coercion you destroy the capacity to love which is your very nature, for you cannot but do to others what you allow others to do to you. Contemplate, then, all the control and coercion in your life and hopefully this contemplation alone will cause them to drop. The moment they drop, freedom will arise. And freedom is just another word for love.

11

You Will Truly Serve Only What You Love

Stephen Colbert

Okay, you have been told to follow your dreams. But what if it's a stupid dream? For instance Stephen Colbert of twenty-five years ago lived at 2015 North Ridge—with two men and three women—in what I now know was a brothel. He dreamed of living alone—well, alone with his beard—in a large, barren, loft apartment—lots of blond wood—wearing a kimono, with a futon on the floor, and a samovar of tea constantly bubbling in the background, doing Shakespeare in the street for the homeless. Today, I am a beardless, suburban dad who lives in a house, wears no-iron khakis, and makes Anthony Wiener jokes for a living. And I love it. Because thankfully dreams can change. If we'd all stuck with our first dream, the world would be overrun with cowboys and princesses.

So whatever your dream is right now, if you don't achieve it, you haven't failed, and you're not some loser.

But just as importantly—and this is the part I may not get right, and you may not listen to—if you do get your dream, you are not a winner.

After I graduated from here, I moved down to Chicago and did improv. Now there are very few rules to improvisation, but one of the things I was taught early on is that you are not the most important person in the scene. Everybody else is. And if they are the most important people in the scene, you will naturally pay attention to them and serve them. But the good news is you're in the scene too. So hopefully to them you're the most important person, and they will serve you. No one is leading, you're all following the follower, serving the servant. You cannot win improv.

And life is an improvisation. You have no idea what's going to happen next and you are mostly just making things up as you go along.

And like improv, you cannot win your life.

Even when it might look like you're winning. I have my own show, which I love doing. Full of very talented people ready to serve me. And it's great. But at my best, I am serving them just as hard, and together, we serve a common idea, in this case the character Stephen Colbert, who it's clear, isn't interested in serving anyone. And a sure sign that things are going well is when no one can really remember whose idea was whose, or who should get credit for what jokes.

Though naturally I take credit for all of them.

But if we should serve others, and together serve some common goal or idea—for any one you, what is that idea? And who are those people?

In my experience, you will truly serve only what you love, because, as the prophet says, service is love made visible.

If you love friends, you will serve your friends.

If you love community, you will serve your community.

If you love money, you will serve your money.

And if you love only yourself, you will serve only yourself. And you will have only yourself.

So no more winning. Instead, try to love others and serve others, and hopefully find those who love and serve you in return.

In closing, I'd like to apologize for being predictable. The *New York Times* has analyzed the hundreds of commencement speeches given so far in 2011, and found that "love," and "service" were two of the most used words.

I can only hope that because of my speech today, the word "brothel" comes in a close third.

12

Justice Is What Love Looks Like In Public

Philip Walsh

In my public life, I find myself talking a lot about issues of justice and equity. But I have long reflected on the fact that at the end of the day, when I go home to my wife and three daughters, the language of "justice" and "equity" morphs into the language of love, compassion, and kindness.

I never say to my daughter: "Please be more just with your sister." Or, "Be more equitable with her." I only speak in the language of love: "Love your sister." "Be kind to her."

I have long thought that this is because we are conditioned to be somewhat squeamish, even ambivalent, about love. There is a sense that love is sentimental, romantic, irrational. It is unpredictable and fickle. It makes us weak. It causes us to do things that are out of character, like watching sappy movies and leaking out of our eyes. In part due to these reasons, I think, we don't hear much about love in our politics and our other public discourse. Too much talk about love and one starts to lose credibility. Becomes soft.

Now, however, as I reflect on all of this violence around us—domestic violence, racialized violence, political violence, gun violence, sectarian violence—I think it goes deeper than that.

Our domestic language of love is accompanied by an implicit understanding of—and belief in—the essential worth and dignity of the other. We don't fall back on the language of "justice" and "equity" in our domestic lives because we acknowledge and accept our responsibility to love our family members, even if we don't always like them.

Which leads me to ask:

What would happen if we rejected this bifurcated language that requires the transactional, sanitized language of justice and equity in public and reserves our lexicon about love for the privacy of our domestic lives?

What would happen to us and with us if we brought our love out into the public? What would that look like? What would we become?

How would we be transformed, individually and collectively, if we agreed to acknowledge and accept the intrinsic dignity, value, and worth of our neighbor? And not only the next door neighbor who we like and looks like us, but also the other neighbor who looks weird and talks funny.

And the Black Lives Matter activist.

And the police officer.

What if we loved them, even if we suspected we might not like them? I suspect we would learn the lesson that families teach so efficiently: that like is not a pre-condition for love, though it is often the result.

As I reflect on these themes, I recall three distinct political philosophers who, each in their unique way, exhort us to embrace a far more aggressive role for love in our public lives.

"Justice," says Dr. Cornel West, "is what love looks like in public."

Jesus instructed his disciples to "love your neighbor as yourself," affirming that there was no greater commandment.

Dr. Martin Luther King Jr. spoke of the "beloved community," not as a utopic vision, but as a uniquely transformational force in our relationships and our communities.

You don't have to agree with all of them, because they all agree with each other:

Love is not soft, but strong and difficult and transformative.

And it is a radical, profound, and deeply necessary social and political act. Especially today.

13

Love and the Purpose of Life

Mother Teresa

We have not come into the world to be numbered; we have been created for a purpose; for great things: to love and be loved.

Jesus said love one another. He didn't say love the whole world. I never look at the masses as my responsibility. I look at the individual. I can love only one person at a time. I can feed only one person at a time. Just one, one, one. It is not how much we do, but how much love we put in the doing. It is not how much we give, but how much love we put in the giving. Do ordinary things with extraordinary love.

The fruit of love is service, which is compassion in action. Love is a fruit in season at all times, and within reach of every hand. If we pray, we will believe; if we believe, we will love; if we love, we will serve. Whenever you share love with others, you'll notice the peace that comes to you and to them.

Spread love everywhere you go. Let no one ever come to you without leaving happier. Joy is a net of love in which you can catch souls. The hunger for love is much more difficult to remove than the hunger for bread. Do not think that love in order to be genuine has to be extraordinary. What we need is to love without getting tired. Be faithful in small things because it is in them that your strength lies. Do not wait for leaders; do it alone, person to person.

At the heart of silence is prayer. At the heart of prayer is faith. At the heart of faith is life. At the heart of life is service. Love cannot remain by itself—it has no meaning. Love has to be put into action, and that action is service. Work without love is slavery.

Let no one ever come to you without leaving better and happier. Be the living expression of God's kindness: kindness in your face, kindness in your eyes, kindness in your smile. Smile at each other. Smile at your wife, smile at your husband, smile at your children, smile at each other—it doesn't matter who it is—and that will help you to grow up in greater love for each other. Every time you smile at someone, it is an action of love, a gift to that person, a beautiful thing.

The greatest disease in the West today is not TB or leprosy; it is being unwanted, unloved, and uncared for. We can cure physical diseases with medicine, but the only cure for loneliness, despair, and hopelessness is love. There are many in the world who are dying for a piece of bread, but there are many more dying for a little love. The poverty in the West is a different kind of poverty—it is not only a poverty of loneliness but also of spirituality. There's a hunger for love, as there is a hunger for God.

If you are humble nothing will touch you, neither praise nor disgrace, because you know what you are. These are the few ways we can practice humility: to speak as little as possible of one's self; to mind one's own business; not to want to manage other people's affairs; to avoid curiosity; to accept contradictions and correction cheerfully; to pass over the mistakes of others; to accept insults and injuries; to accept being slighted, forgotten and disliked; to be kind and gentle even under provocation; never to stand on one's dignity; to choose always the hardest.

I am not sure exactly what heaven will be like, but I know that when we die and it comes time for God to judge us, he will not ask, "How many good things have you done in your life?" rather he will ask, "How much love did you put into what you did?"

> *Life is a song, sing it.*
> *Life is a struggle, accept it.*
> *Life is an opportunity, benefit from it.*
> *Life is beauty, admire it.*
> *Life is a dream, realize it.*
> *Life is love, enjoy it.*
> *Life is mystery, know it.*
> *Life is a promise, fulfill it.*
> *Life is a game, play it. . . .*
> *Life is an adventure, dare it.*
> *Life is too precious, do not destroy it.*

Love Notes

Love is the only sane and satisfac-
tory answer to the problem of human
existence.

—ERICH FROMM

Life is suffering
Love is the desire to see unnecessary
suffering ameliorated.
Truth is the handmaiden of love.
Dialogue is the pathway to truth.
Humility is recognition of personal
insufficiency and the willingness to learn.
To learn is to die voluntarily and be
born again, in great ways and small.
So speech must be untrammeled.
So that dialogue can take place.
So that we can all humbly learn.
So that truth can serve love.
So that suffering can be ameliorated.

THE WAY OF LOVE

*So that we can all stumble forward to
the Kingdom of God.*

—JORDAN PETERSON

*The more one forgets himself—by giv-
ing himself to a cause to serve or another person to love—the more human
he is and the more he actualizes himself. What is called self-actualization
is not an attainable aim at all, for the
simple reason that the more one would
strive for it, the more he would miss
it. In other words, self-actualization
is possible only as a side-effect of self-
transcendence.*

—VICTOR FRANKL

*I know for sure that love saves me and
that it is here to save us all.*

—MAYA ANGELOU

14

The Daring Adventure of Love

Ilia Delio

Life in God should be a daring adventure of love—a continuous journey of putting aside our securities to enter more profoundly into the uncharted depths of God. Too often, however, we settle for mediocrity. We follow the rules and practices of prayer but we are unwilling or, for various reasons, unable to give ourselves totally to God. To settle on the plain of mediocrity is really to settle for something less than God that leaves the heart restless and unfulfilled. A story from the desert fathers reminds us that giving oneself wholly to God can make a difference: Abba Lot went to see Abba Joseph and said to him, "Abba, as far as I can I say my little office, I fast a little, I pray and meditate, I live in peace and as far as I can, I purify my thoughts. What else can I do?" Then the old man stood up and stretched his hands towards heaven. His fingers became like ten lamps of fire and he said to him, "If you will, you can become all flame."

> *Love is always a little tipsy and falling over*
> *   itself.*
> *God is like that. That absolute being in love,*
> *always a little tipsy, always falling over*
> *   God's self*
> *to share that love within other.*

In the end, the only thing that will matter will be how well we loved. If the pandemic has taught us anything, it is to pay attention to the person we encounter, more so, to be attentive to the ones we love (and often take for granted). To be present in the moment, heart and soul, attentive to the sounds of life in the midst of anxiety, laughter, sorrow, and wonder. Heaven opens where we are and invites us in as we are. The moral of the story is that grace is everywhere and love abounds, but it must be received and celebrated. This is the sacrament of everyday life.

15

Love Is for Living

Carlo Carretto

Having convinced myself of the primacy of charity, having become aware that in touching charity I am touching God, that in living charity I am living God in me, I must this evening, before finishing my meditation, look at tomorrow to subject it to this light and live it out under the inspiration of this synthesis of love. Basically I must do what Jesus—who brought God's love to earth and communicated it to us—would do in my position. I must remember that the opportunities I shall have to suffer, to pardon, to accept are treasures not to be lost through distraction and values that I must make my own as a worthy response to God's plan in creation.

My life is worth living if I can learn to transform everything that happens to me into love, in imitation of Jesus: because love is for living.

When I meet a brother of mine who has caused me great pain in the past by viciously calumniating me, I shall love him, and in loving him I shall transform the evil done to me into good: because love is for living.

When I have to live with people who do not see things the same way I see them, who say they are enemies of my faith, I shall love them, and in loving them I shall sow the seeds of future dialogue in my heart and theirs: because love is for living.

When I go into a shop to buy something for myself—clothes, food, or whatever it may be—I shall think of my brothers and sisters who are poorer than I am, of the hungry and the naked, and I shall use this thought to govern my purchases, trying out of love to be tight with myself and generous with them: because love is for living.

When I see time's destructive traces in my body and the approach of old age, I shall try to love even more in order to transform the coldest season of life into a total gift of myself in preparation for the imminent holocaust: because love is for living.

When I see the evening of my life, or, on the pavement in a car accident, in the agony of a fatal illness, in the ward of a geriatric hospital, feel the end coming, I shall reach out again for love, striving to accept in joy whatever fate God has had in store for me: because love is for living.

Yes, love is God in me, and if I am in love I am in God, that is, in life, in grace: a sharer in God's being. . . .

If charity is God in me, why look for God any further than myself?

And if God is in me as love, why do I change or disfigure God's face with acts or values which are not love?

16

Love Is Mysterious

Jack Kornfield

Love is mysterious. We don't know what it is, but we know when it is present. If we seek love, we must ask where it is to be found. It is here only in this moment. To love in the past is simply a memory. To love in the future is a fantasy. There is only one place where love can be found, where intimacy and awakening can be found, and that is in the present. When we live in our thoughts of the past and future, everything seems distant, hurried, or unfulfilled. The only place we can genuinely love a tree, the sky, a child, or our lover is in the here and now. Emily Dickinson wrote, "'Til the first friend dies, we think ecstasy impersonal, but then discover that he was the cup from which we drank it, itself as yet unknown." Only in the intimacy of the timeless present can we awaken. This intimacy connects us to one another, allows us to belong, and in this belonging, we experience love. In this we move beyond our separateness, our contraction, our limited sense of ourselves.

If we investigate what keeps us from intimacy, what keeps us from love, we will discover it is always an expectation, a hope, a thought, or a fantasy. It is the same expectation that keeps us from awakening. Awakening is not far away; it is nearer than near. As it says in the Buddhist texts, "Awakening is not something newly discovered; it has always existed. There is no need to seek or follow the advice of others. Learn to listen to that voice within yourself just here and now. Your body and mind will become clear and you will realize the unity of all things. Do not doubt the possibilities because of the simplicity of these teachings. If you can't find the truth right where you are, where else do you think you will find it?"

There are many words for awakening and many expressions of love offered to us in great spiritual teachings. There are expressions of love in action as enlightened activity. There are expressions of enlightenment as silence, and love as heartfelt understanding. There are expressions of awakening as freedom in the realms of form and as that which lies beyond all form. In Buddhism enlightenment is called the unconditioned, that which shines naturally when the heart is not entangled in the forces of grasping, hatred, and ignorance. When the heart is free of these forces, true intimacy and love exist. There is an awakening in the midst of all things, a love that can touch and include all things, a freedom and fearlessness that can enter every realm. In this we do not remove ourselves from life but rest in the very center of it. In this we are able to be intimate with all things.

17

Love Sails Me around the House

Thomas Merton

Love sails me around the house. I walk two steps on the ground and four steps in the air. It is love. It is consolation. I don't care if it is consolation. I am not attached to consolation. I love God. Love carries me all around. I don't want to do anything but love.

And when the bell rings, it is like pulling teeth to make myself shift because of that love, secret love, hidden love, obscure love, down inside me and outside me, where I don't care to talk about it. Anyway, I don't have the time or the energy to discuss such matters. I have only time for eternity, which is to say, for love, love, love.

Maybe Saint Teresa would like to have me snap out of it, but it is pure, I tell you: I am not attached to it (I hope) and it is love, and it gives me soft punches all the time in the center of my heart. Love is pushing me around the monastery, love is kicking me all around like a gong, I tell you. Love is the only thing that makes it possible for me to continue to tick.

Love Notes

*Love takes off the masks that we fear
we cannot live without and know we
cannot live within. I use the word
"love" here not merely in the personal
sense but as a state of being, or a state
of grace—not in the infantile American
sense of being made happy but in the
tough and universal sense of quest and
daring and growth.*

—JAMES BALDWIN

*Love makes your soul crawl out from
its hiding place.*

—ZORA NEALE HURSTON

*Love in action is a harsh and dreadful
thing compared to love in dreams.*

—FYODOR DOSTOEVSKY

The Way of Love

*All you need is love. But a little choco-
late now and then doesn't hurt.*

—Charles M. Schulz

What Is This Thing Called Love?

Matthew Fox

Given the coronavirus that has killed more than four million human beings and the promise from scientists that more such viruses are on their way, and given the almost daily news of the effects of climate change on the oceans, glaciers, sources of water, wildfires, hurricanes of increased frequency and velocity, and given the millions of species going extinct, it is not an exaggeration to propose that we are living in an apocalyptic time.

The human experiment faces a dire challenge. Questions jump to mind: Are we humans going extinct? What does it mean to be a human being? What is this thing called love? What does it mean to say "God is love"? Have we failed, has religion failed, has God failed, in an attempt to teach us love? Is there time left to uncover and practice a deeper love, one that can assist the saving of the earth, ourselves, and other creatures on our unique but imperiled planet? Have we been misunderstanding what love means?

When I consider what the great mystics say about love, it does seem to me that we have been both misunderstanding it—and misdefining it—for a long time. Our greatest mistake has been our narcissism—we think it is about us and our mates. A kind of soap opera love so anthropocentric that it has left out our relationship to the sun and moon, the earth and sky, the trees and oceans, rivers and lakes, soil and animals that have made our species possible and upon whom we depend for just about everything. Consider the words of Caribbean poet Derek Walcott who, on accepting the Nobel prize for poetry in 1972, said this in his acceptance speech: "The fate of poetry is to fall in love with the world in spite of history." Have we done that yet? If we had, would Mother Earth be as endangered as she is? Is there still time?

In the Middle Ages, which began philosophy not with the human but with the cosmos, the great mystics insisted that the whole—the cosmos and the earth—are the starting point for love. "We were loved before the beginning" pronounced Julian of Norwich, and of course today's science confirms that, insofar as the universe unfolded for a good 13.8 billion years before Earth was ready to welcome our species. Over that lengthy period, so much evolution had to take place to set the table for our existence, including the supernova explosion that birthed the sun and elements of our bodies of which we and stars are made, the placement of the moon, and so much more. Have we remembered to thank all these creatures for our existence?

Julian of Norwich, like other medieval mystics, places love in a cosmic context. One day she received a vision: "God showed me in my palm a little thing round as a ball about the size of a hazelnut. I looked at it with the eye of my understanding and asked myself: 'What is this thing?' And I was answered: 'It is everything that is created.' I wondered how it could survive, since it seemed so little it could suddenly disintegrate into nothing. The answer came: 'It endures and ever will endure, because God loves it.' And so everything has being because of God's love."

This is truly a story of cosmic love which is God's kind of love. Are we imitating God?

Meister Eckhart also recognizes love in a cosmic and earth context when he says the human soul is as mysterious and "unfathomable" as God is. And that "the best name for God is compassion." Compassion has a cosmic dimension to it. "The highest work of God is compassion and this means that God sets the soul in the highest and purest place which it can occupy: in space, in the sea, in a fathomless ocean; and there God works compassion. Therefore, the prophet says: 'Lord, have compassion on the people who are in you.' What people are in God? Saint John says: 'God is love and whoever remains in love remains in God and God in him' (1 Jn. 4:16)."

Again, we see and feel here the immensity of a cosmic compassion, bigger than a "fathomless ocean," in which we swim, move and have our being. Eckhart actually defines the very meaning of the human soul as compassion when he declares that "the soul is where God works compassion."

Compassion is not just a state of being for Eckhart. It is also a practice, a doing. "Compassion means justice," he insists, drawing from the wisdom of the prophets of Israel. Making justice happen is work, God's work. God rejoices "at every work of the just person, however small it is. When this work is done through justice and results in justice, God will rejoice at it, indeed, God will rejoice through and through; for nothing remains in his ground which does not tickle him through and through out of joy." There is no love without justice—this is Eckhart's teaching and that of the prophets of Israel.

Including justice in our understanding of love is integral to Jewish teaching, and therefore that of Jesus. Mexican theologian José Miranda warns us that to have split love from justice has been a "disastrous error" in Christianity. Authentic love interferes with all soap opera talk of love which reeks of sentimentalism (behind which violence always lurks, according to Carl Jung). Sentimentalism is "the political sense gone rancid" and inherent to it is titillation, "exhibition and commercialization of the self . . . [that] cannot exist without an audience," as Anne Douglas puts it. Justice is absent. Sentimentalism has dominated popular culture in America for over 150 years, and upholds an economic system of consumerism. It is not love but a smothering of love/justice under an idolatrous consumerism—a lust for objects, not relationships.

There is another way. The way of love/justice. We can do better.

19

This Is Love, Become Love, Be That One

Eckhart Tolle, Meister Eckhart, and Sheri Bessi-Eckert

This Is Love

Eckhart Tolle

Love is a state of being. Your love is not outside; it is deep within you. You can never lose it, and it cannot leave you. It is not dependent on some other body, some external form. In the stillness of your presence, you can feel your own formless and timeless reality as the unmanifested life that animates your physical form. You can then feel the same life deep within every other human and every other creature. You look beyond the veil of form and separation. This is the realization of oneness. This is love.

Become Love

Meister Eckhart

If you want to know God, become love.
If you want to know others, become love.
If you want to know yourself, become love.
And if you want to know love,
forget all you thought you knew or needed to know,
and become love.

Be That One

Sheri Bessi-Eckert

Be that one. That one who forgives when deep offense
has been committed. That one who loves when no one
else does. That one who gives kindness to those who are
mean. Be that one who looks past the insult. Instead seeing the pain that motivated it. That one who shines light
upon those who sit in utter darkness. Because the impact
of being that one runs far and wide. It brings healing to
the wounded, joy to the sad, and hope to those in despair.
Be that one.

20

The Power of Love
(or Imagine a World Where Love Is the Way)

Bishop Michael Curry

Bishop Michael Curry, the first African American presiding bishop of the Episcopal Church in the United States gave the sermon during the wedding ceremony of Britain's Prince Harry and Meghan Markle. These are excerpts.

The late Dr. Martin Luther King Jr once said, and I quote: "We must discover the power of love, the redemptive power of love. And when we do that, we will make of this old world a new world, for love is the only way."

There's power in love. Don't underestimate it. Don't even over-sentimentalize it. There's power, power in love.

And there's a reason for it. The reason has to do with the source. We were made by a power of love, and our lives were meant—and are meant—to be lived in that love. That's why we are here.

Ultimately, the source of love is God himself: the source of all of our lives. There's an old medieval poem that says: "Where true love is found, God himself is there."

The New Testament says it this way: "Beloved, let us love one another, because love is of God, and those who love are born of God and know God. Those who do not love do not know God."

Why? For God is love.

There's power in love. There's power in love to help and heal when nothing else can.

There's power in love to lift up and liberate when nothing else will.

There's power in love to show us the way to live.

Think and imagine a world where love is the way.

Imagine our homes and families where love is the way. Imagine neighborhoods and communities where love is the way.

Imagine governments and nations where love is the way. Imagine business and commerce where love is the way.

Imagine this tired old world where love is the way. When love is the way—unselfish, sacrificial, redemptive.

When love is the way, then no child will go to bed hungry in this world ever again.

When love is the way, we will let justice roll down like a mighty stream and righteousness like an ever-flowing brook.

When love is the way, poverty will become history. When love is the way, the earth will be a sanctuary.

When love is the way, we will lay down our swords and shields, down by the riverside, to study war no more.

When love is the way, there's plenty good room—plenty good room—for all of God's children.

Because when love is the way, we actually treat each other, well . . . like we are actually family.

When love is the way, we know that God is the source of us all, and we are brothers and sisters, children of God.

My brothers and sisters, that's a new heaven, a new earth, a new world, a new human family.

Dr. King was right: we must discover love—the redemptive power of love. And when we do that, we will make of this old world, a new world.

My brother, my sister, God love you, God bless you, and may God hold us all in those almighty hands of love.

PART TWO

LOVE OF GOD

We love because God first loved us.

*—*1 JOHN 4:19

May We Remember That God Is the Only Love

Donna Goddard

May we be grateful for everything good.
Good IS everything.
May we remember that God is the only Love.
May our eyes radiate nonconditional benevolence.
May our awareness be of spiritual perfection.
May our freedom be boundless.
May we know the loveliness of love.
May the Divine presence fill our consciousness.
May we feel the magnificent capacity of Life.
May our touch be uplifting.
May our influence be a blessing.
May we feel the immensity of Divinity.
May we know the sublime Love that we are part of.
May it sustain us.
It IS us.

What Do I Love When I Love God

St. Augustine

What is it then that I love when I love you? Not bodily beauty, and not temporal glory, not the clear shining light, lovely as it is to our eyes, not the sweet melodies of many-moded songs, nor the soft smell of flowers and ointments and perfumes, not manna and honey, not limbs made for the body's embrace, not these do I love when I love my God. Yet I do love a certain voice, a certain odor, a certain food, a certain embrace when I love my God; a light, a voice, an odor, a food, an embrace for the man within me, where his light, which no place can contain floods into my soul; where he utters words that time does not speed away; where he sends forth an aroma that no wind can scatter; where he provides food that no eating can lessen, where he so clings that satiety does not sunder us. This is what I love when I love my God.

God's Signature

Ernesto Cardenal

God's signature is on the whole of nature. All creatures are love letters from God to us. They are outbursts of love. The whole of nature is bursting with love, set in it by God, who is love, to kindle the fire of love in us. All things have no other reason for existing, no other meaning. They can give us no satisfaction or pleasure beyond this, to stir in us the love of God.

Nature is like God's shadow, reflecting God's beauty and splendor. The quiet blue lake has the splendor of God. God's fingerprints are upon every particle of matter. In every atom is an image of the Trinity, the figure of the triune God. That is why God's creation so fills us with enthusiasm.

And my body was also made for the love of God. Every cell in my body is a hymn to my creator and a declaration of love.

As the kingfisher was made to fish and the humming bird to suck nectar from flowers, so we were made for contemplation and love of God.

Start with Loving a Stone

Richard Rohr

Once upon a time, a small Jewish boy went to his rabbi and said he didn't know how to love God. "How can I love God when I've never seen him?" asked the boy. "I think I understand how to love my mother, my father, my brother, my little sister, and even the people in our neighborhood, but I don't know how I'm supposed to love God."

The rabbi looked at the little boy and said, "Start with a stone. Try to love a stone. Try to be present to the most simple and basic thing in reality so you can see its goodness and beauty. Then let that goodness and beauty come into you. Let it speak to you. Start with a stone." The boy nodded with understanding.

"Then, when you can love a stone," the rabbi continued, "try a flower. See if you can love a flower. See if you can be present to it and let its beauty come into you. See if you can let its life come into you and you can give yourself to it. You don't have to pluck it, possess it, or destroy it. You can just love it over there in the garden." The boy nodded again.

"I'm not saying it's wrong to pick flowers," added the rabbi. "I'm just asking you to learn something from the flower without putting it in a vase." The boy smiled, which meant he understood—or maybe he didn't. Just in case he didn't, the rabbi chose the boy's pet dog as the next object of loving and listening. The boy nodded and smiled when the rabbi talked about his dog; he even said, "Yes, Rabbi."

"Then," the rabbi went on, "try to love the sky and the mountains, the beauty of all creation. Try to be present to it in its many forms. Let it speak to you and let it come into you." The boy sensed the rabbi wanted to say some more, so he nodded again, as if he understood.

"Then," the rabbi said, "try to love a woman. Try to be faithful to a woman and sacrifice yourself for her. After you have loved a stone, a flower, your little dog, the mountain, the sky, and a woman, then you'll be ready to love God."

25

God Is the Ocean in Which We All Swim

Patrick T. Reardon

I have gotten to a point that I can't go along anymore with Michelangelo's God on the ceiling of the Sistine Chapel. Great art, but, gee, God as an old guy with a long gray beard? No thanks.

For a long time, my wife Cathy has had her own spin on this. At Mass, when the celebrants starts, "Our Father . . . ," Cathy adds in a loud voice, " . . . and Mother."

That makes more sense, but it still doesn't do the job for me. I am able to think of God like a parent, loving me and wanting what's best for me and providing me with what I need to live a full life and, again like a good parent, giving me the space I need to fail and learn from my failures.

What doesn't work for me is the idea that if something good happens, it's God up in heaven pulling the strings. Say I'm running to the airport, late for a flight, and against all odds, I get on the flight. I can't think that God made that happen. And I can't find it in me to pray to God to make that happen.

If I think God is dipping into my life to make it possible for me to get on the flight, what am I to think if I land, get a rental car and, within 20 minutes, I'm in an accident? Did God pull some string to make that happen? Or did God fail to pull the right string?

Things happen in life, good and bad. Good things happen to bad people. Bad things happen to good people. Life isn't fair as anyone knows who has come to the realization, as humans must, that we are born to die. You and I live under a death sentence.

In recent years, Job has become one of my heroes. You know, the guy in the Bible who is afflicted with a whole lot of bad stuff, the guy known for "the patience of Job."

Job, however, is anything but patient. He whines to God and complains and says a lot of "woe is me." His faith never wavers—that's where the "patience" comes in—but he browbeats God, demanding why, as a good guy, he has to put up with all these disasters, fires and boils, as well as the dung heap where he lives.

Finally, enough is enough, and "out of the storm," sounding more than a little exasperated, God says: "Where were you when I founded the Earth? Tell me, if you have understanding. . . . Have you ever in your lifetime commanded the morning and shown the dawn its place?"

We are all connected inextricably because we exist in the same water and find our sustenance in this ocean and everything else we need to live.

God goes on like that for 71 verses, and, basically, God is saying to Job, "Come on, I'm God, and you're not. I understand this stuff, and you don't."

This has been very comforting to me. I don't know about you, but life completely mystifies me. I try to figure it out, and I come up with ways in which to frame things and find meaning. But I'm always adjusting these, and they're never adequate.

What's comforting is that, even if I don't understand life, God does. Just like the flower doesn't understand the storm that is pounding it with rain and buffeting it with wind, I am trying to bloom in the storm of life.

Then, during a recent therapy session in which I was talking about my nephew's widespread cancer and of the deaths that are happening all around me, I was a bit taken aback when my therapist asked, "Where does God fit in all this?"

After fumbling around a bit, what I came up with, essentially, is that I see God as the ocean we all swim in.

We're all in this ocean whether we realize it or not. (Does the shark know it's in an ocean?) We are all connected inextricably because we exist in the same water and find our sustenance in this ocean and everything else we need to live.

So, then, spinning this out, I took the same image and said that religious faith (or any faith in something that gives life meaning) is the ocean in which we all swim, whether we realize it or not.

In thinking this, am I thinking that God and faith are the same? I think so.

So then I went to love, meaning the whole array of connections in which we touch each other and are touched—*love* is the ocean in which we all swim.

After all, we are individuals, but we exist among others. Even hermits once lived among others, and even as a hermit lives in isolation, he or she breathes the same air and sees the same sun as the rest of humanity.

St. Paul tells us that God is love, so thinking about God and love being the same ocean in which we all swim makes sense—and faith being that ocean too.

Where, the theologically inclined may ask, is God as a person, a foundation of Christianity? My thought is that God is a person and an ocean in a way that I can't understand because, well, I'm not God.

None of this, of course, pushes the human being who was and is Jesus off the stage. Jesus is still in the center of faith and love while also being God.

Despite 2,000 years of theological theorizing, I think it's safe to say no one understands how Jesus can be a human being and also be God.

So maybe I'm not so crazy to think of God as a person and as an ocean.

><

> *We are not a drop in the ocean.*
> *We are the entire ocean in one drop.*
>
> —RUMI

Our Love Flows
from the Love of God

Søren Kierkegaard

As the calm lake stems from the deep spring that no eye saw, so too a person's love has a still deeper ground, in God's love. If there were no gushing spring at the bottom, if God were not love, then neither would there be the little lake nor either a person's love. As the calm lake stems darkly from the deep spring, so a person's love originates mysteriously in God's. As the calm lake indeed invites you to contemplate it, yet with the darkness of the reflection prevents you from seeing through it, so does love's mysterious origin in God's love prevent you from seeing its ground. When you think you see it, it is a reflection that deceives you, as if what only hides the deeper ground were itself the ground.

This is all I have known for certain, that God is love. Even if I have been mistaken on this or that fine point,

God is nevertheless love. If I have made a mistake, it will be plain enough; so I repent—and God is love. He is love, not he was love, nor, he will be love, oh no, even that future was too slow for me, he is love. Oh, how wonderful. Sometimes, perhaps, my repentance does not come at once, and so there is a future. But God keeps no person waiting, he is love. Like spring-water which keeps the same temperature summer and winter—so is God's love. His love is a spring that never runs dry.

Love Notes

God is love.

—1 JOHN 4:16

*We live and move and have our being
in God (Love). As some of your own
poets have said, "We are his offspring."*

—ACTS 17:28

*God made us in his own image and
likeness.*

—GENESIS 1:26

*And God saw all that he had made,
and behold, it was very good.*

—GENESIS 1:31

*Love all God's creation, both the whole
and every grain of sand. Love every leaf,*

every ray of light. Love the animals, love the plants, love each separate thing. If you love each thing, you will perceive the mystery of God in all; and when once you perceive this, you will grow every day to a fuller understanding of it, until you come at last to love the whole world with a love that will be all-embracing and universal.

—Fyodor Dostoevsky

So above all, be loving. This ties everything together perfectly.

—Colossians 3:14

27

We Love Because He First Loved Us

Robert Ellsberg

One of the paradoxes of the gospel is the teaching that we truly possess only what we give away. Love that hinges on the expectation of return is simply the law of the marketplace or what Simone Weil liked to call gravity. True love defies the laws of gravity; it does not express itself through grasping, but through freely giving. . . .

In the Gospel of Luke, Jesus observes a man named Zacchaeus who has climbed a sycamore tree to get a better view over the crowd. Zacchaeus is a short man, but he has another reason for observing from afar. He is a tax collector, a man disdained by his neighbors as a social parasite. Nevertheless, from the midst of the crowd Jesus calls him down from his sycamore tree, addressing him by name: "Zacchaeus, make haste and come down; for I must stay at your house today." The crowd mumbles scornfully; Zacchaeus is a sinner. But Zacchaeus is so moved by this personal attention that he responds with a bold public declaration: He will change his life; he will give half his property to the poor; he will restore the goods of anyone he has defrauded (Luke 19:1–8).

Many of the saints could identify with that man in the sycamore tree. Like Zacchaeus, they had the experience of being known and loved by God. In this love they found the courage to start anew, to do impossible things, to become different people. As St. John the Evangelist wrote, "We love, because he first loved us" (1 John 4:19).

28

I Am Sustained by the Love of God

A Course in Miracles

Here is the answer to every problem that will confront you, today and tomorrow and throughout time. In this world, you believe you are sustained by everything but God. Your faith is placed in the most trivial and insane symbols; pills, money, "protective" clothing, influence, prestige, being liked, knowing the "right" people, and an endless list of forms of nothingness that you endow with magical powers.

All these things are your replacements for the Love of God. All these things are cherished to ensure a body identification. They are songs of praise to the ego. Do not put your faith in the worthless. It will not sustain you.

Only the Love of God will protect you in all circumstances. It will lift you out of every trial, and raise you high above all the perceived dangers of this world into a climate of perfect peace and safety. It will transport you into a state of mind that nothing can threaten, nothing can disturb, and where nothing can intrude upon the eternal calm of the Son of God.

Put not your faith in illusions. They will fail you. Put all your faith in the Love of God within you; eternal, changeless, and forever unfailing. This is the answer to whatever confronts you today. Through the Love of God within you, you can resolve all seeming difficulties without effort and in sure confidence. Tell yourself this often today. It is a declaration of release from the belief in idols. It is your acknowledgment of the truth about yourself.

≻≈⊂

29

God Is a Mother, Too

Vickie Leach

I was fifteen months old, a happy carefree kid . . . until the day I fell. It was a bad fall. I landed on a glass rabbit which cut my eye badly enough to blind it. Trying to save the eye, the doctors stitched the eyeball together where it was cut, leaving a big ugly scar in the middle of my eye. The attempt failed, but my mama, in all of her wisdom, found a doctor who knew that if the eye were removed entirely, my face would grow up badly distorted, so my scarred, sightless, cloudy and gray eye lived on with me. And as I grew, this sightless eye in so many ways controlled me.

I walked with my face looking at the floor so people would not see the ugly me. Sometimes people, even strangers, asked me embarrassing questions or made hurtful remarks. When the kids played games, I was always the "monster." I grew up imagining that everyone looked at me with disdain, as if my appearance were my fault. I always felt like I was a freak.

Yet Mama would say to me, at every turn, "Hold your head up high and face the world." It became a litany that I relied on. She had started when I was young. She would hold me in her arms and stroke my hair and say, "If you hold your head up, it will be okay, and people will see your beautiful soul." She continued this message whenever I wanted to hide.

Those words have meant different things to me over the years. As a little child, I thought Mama meant, "Be careful or you will fall down or bump into something because you are not looking." As an adolescent, even though I tended to look down to hide my shame, I found that sometimes when I held my head up and let people know me, they liked me. My mama's words helped me to begin to realize that by letting people look at my face, I let them recognize the intelligence and beauty behind both eyes even if they couldn't see it on the surface.

In high school I was successful both academically and socially. I was even elected class president, but on the inside I still felt like a freak. All I really wanted was to look like everyone else. When things got really bad, I would cry to my mama and she would look at me with loving eyes and say, "Hold your head up high and face the world. Let them see the beauty that is inside."

When I met the man who would become my partner for life, we looked each other straight in the eye, and he told me I was beautiful inside and out. He meant it. My mama's love and encouragement were the spark that gave me the confidence to overcome my own doubt. I had faced adversity, encountered my problems head on, and learned not only to appreciate myself but to have deep compassion for others.

"Hold your head up high" has been heard many times in my home. Each of my children has felt its invitation. The gift my mama gave me lives on in another generation.

～

We are all meant to be mothers of God.
—Meister Eckhart

30

God Is My Everything

Thea Bowman

God is bread when you're hungry, water when you're thirsty, a harbor from the storm. God's father to the fatherless, a mother to the motherless. God's my sister, my brother, my leader, my guide, my teacher, my comforter, my friend. God's the way-maker and burden-bearer, a heart-fixer and a mind-regulator. God's my doctor who never lost a patient, my lawyer who never lost a case, my captain who never lost a battle. God's my all in all, my everything.

God's my rock, my sword, my shield, my lily of the valley, my pearl of great price. God's a god of peace and a god of war. Counselor, Emmanuel, Redeemer, Savior, Prince of Peace, Son of God, Mary's little baby, wonderful Word of God.

Love Notes

We see God through the same eye God
sees us. Our eye and God's eye are
one—one seeing, one knowing, one love.
—Meister Eckhart

God sees not as man sees, for man
looks at the outward appearance, but
the Lord looks at the heart.
—1 Samuel 16:7

I say more: the just man justices;
Keeps grace: that keeps all his goings
graces;
Acts in God's eye what in God's eye
he is—
Christ. For Christ plays in ten thou-
sand places,

Love Notes

Lovely in limbs, and lovely in eyes not his
To the father through the features of
men's faces.

—Gerard Manley Hopkins

Each time we look upon the poor, on
the farmworkers who harvest the cof-
fee, the sugarcane, or the cotton or the
farmer who joins the caravan of workers
looking to earn their savings for the
year . . . remember, there is the face of
Christ. . . . The face of Christ is among
the sacks and baskets of the farmwork-
ers; the face of Christ is among those
who are tortured and mistreated in the
prisons; the face of Christ is dying of
hunger in the children who have noth-
ing to eat; the face of Christ is in the
poor who ask the church for their voice
to be heard. How can the church deny
this request when it is Christ who is
telling us to speak for him?

—Óscar Romero

I have now seen the One who sees me.

—Genesis 16:13

89

31

Quick, Open the Door, It's God Coming to Love Us!

Madeleine Delbrêl

We, the ordinary people of the streets, are certain we can love God as much as he might desire to be loved by us.

We don't regard love as something extraordinary, but as something that consumes. We believe that doing little things for God is as much a way of loving him as doing great deeds. Besides, we're not very well informed about the greatness of our acts. There are nevertheless two things we know for sure: first, whatever we do can't help but be small; and second, whatever God does is great.

And so we go about our activities with a sense of great peace.

We know that all our work consists in not shifting about under grace; in not choosing what we would do; and that it is God who acts through us.

There is nothing difficult for God; the one who grows anxious at difficulties is the one who counts on his own capacity for action.

Because we find that love is work enough for us, we don't take the time to categorize what we are doing as either "contemplation" or "action."

We find that prayer is action and that action is prayer. It seems to us that truly loving action is filled with light.

It seems to us that a soul standing before such action is like a night that is full of expectation for the coming dawn. And when the light breaks, when God's will is clearly understood, she lives it out gently, with poise, peacefully watching her God inspiring her and at work within her. It seems to us that action is also an imploring prayer. It does not at all seem to us that action nails us down to our field of work, our apostolate, or our life.

Quite the contrary, we believe that an action perfectly carried out at the time and place it is required of us binds us to the whole Church, sends us out throughout her body, making us available in her.

Our feet march upon a street, but our heartbeat reverberates through the whole world. That is why our small acts, which we can't decide whether they're action or contemplation, perfectly join together the love of God and the love of our neighbor.

Giving ourselves over to his will at the same time gives us over to the Church, whom the same will continuously makes our saving mother of grace.

Each docile act makes us receive God totally and give God totally, in a great freedom of spirit.

And thus life becomes a celebration.

Each tiny act is an extraordinary event, in which heaven is given to us, in which we are able to give heaven to others.

It makes no difference what we do, whether we take in hand a broom or a pen. Whether we speak or keep silent. Whether we are sewing or holding a meeting, caring for a sick person or tapping away at the typewriter.

Whatever it is, it's just the outer shell of an amazing inner reality, the soul's encounter, renewed at each moment, in which, at each moment, the soul grows in grace and becomes ever more beautiful for her God.

Is the doorbell ringing? Quick, open the door! It's God coming to love us. Is someone asking us to do something? Here you are! . . . It's God coming to love us. Is it time to sit down for lunch? Let's go—it's God coming to love us.

Let's let him.

I Love You
for Sentimental Reasons

Marion Amberg

You never know when love will find you. I didn't expect a two-year love affair when I accepted a caregiver assignment with Amy, a ninety-two-year-old Japanese lady in a senior living home. My job was easy: accompany Amy to the dining room for breakfast and dinner, and tuck her into bed at night.

I knew little about Amy's past. I was told that she had grown up in California and that she was imprisoned with her family during World War II at a Japanese internment camp in Colorado. She married and had three children, two sons and a daughter. Her husband had died.

Amy suffered from Alzheimer's. Her mind was diseased, but her soul was whole and full of love. When she first saw me, she burst into song. "I love you . . . for sentimental reasons . . ." She never missed a beat of Nat King Cole's 1946 hit. "I hope you do believe me," she sang on. "I'll give you my heart."

Amy serenaded the nurses and maintenance workers with her song and even feted other residents as she made her way to her table in the dining room. "That's just for you," she'd say, "because I love you."

Many residents snickered behind Amy's back or rolled their eyes. Some pretended not to see or hear her. They still had their "marbles," after all. But Amy was oblivious to it all. She didn't see or hear a thing. The very next day she stopped at their tables and heaped more love on them.

The seasons came and went, but Amy kept on loving. I never figured out how she chose which residents to caress with song. Was it random? Or did she sense a hole in certain hearts? One day an amazing thing happened. Residents stopped being condescending and started smiling at Amy and saying hello. Even John, a crusty old bachelor who liked to complain, fell under her spell.

Doris and Bert and Joanne and Michael began wishing her well. "Have a nice day, Amy! We love you, too!" Sometimes, they even joined her in song. Amy's spirit was like a long planted lilac unexpectedly appearing in spring.

But Alzheimer's was slowly ravaging Amy's brain, and she suffered from bouts of depression and sometimes refused to get out of bed. My fingers untangled her matted hair. "It's time to get dressed and go down for dinner, Amy. Your friends are waiting for you."

"I'm not hungry," she barked, pulling the covers up higher.

And so I would sing. "I love you for sentimental reasons," I crooned as I coaxed her out of bed. Amy peeked at me from under the covers, with a child's smile. She couldn't resist an expression of love.

After a leisurely dinner, we'd return to her apartment, plop down on her blue loveseat, and engage in simple chats. The content rarely changed, but it was Amy's way of making conversation and being sociable, and she liked that time together.

"I love the way you help me," she said, her glasses sliding down her nose. "You're wonderful."

"Not as wonderful as you."

"You're more wonderful!" She slapped my leg in her playful way. "I love you . . . for sentimental reasons." Sometimes her parakeet chirped in too. One day we started harmonizing. I took the soprano part, Amy was contralto. We laughed when I improvised or missed a high note.

Amy loved everybody. And not just for sentimental reasons. Her love was pure. She didn't see race or color or fat or thin or bad behavior. Where had she learned to accept and love others beyond measure? Did her time in the Japanese relocation camp influence her? I'll never know.

Amy's cognitive abilities kept diminishing, and she began withdrawing at times into a secret world.

After helping her for two years, I was sad when they moved her from assisted living to the memory care unit. Amy needed closer monitoring by the nursing staff, and our love fests came to an end. We whooped it up our last night together. We belted out "For Sentimental Reasons" for old times' sake and told each other again how wonderful the other was. But I had learned now that for Amy there was no other. There was only we.

I tucked her into bed for the last time. She told me she loved me.

"I love you more." I leaned in to give her a goodnight kiss on the cheek.

"That's impossible," she beamed. "I love you . . . *forever and ever.*"

My heart stopped. I heard new words but my soul saw one ancient truth. Why didn't I see it sooner? God is love, and God's face has been looking at me for two years.

"I love you, Amy," I whispered, closing the door behind me. "I hope you do believe me. I've given you my heart."

33

God

Brian Doyle

By purest chance I was out in our street when the
    kindergarten
Bus mumbled past going slow and I looked up just as all
    seven
Kids on my side of the bus looked at me and I grinned
    and they
Lit up and all this crap about God being dead and where
    is God
And who owns God and who hears God better than
    whom is the
Most egregiously stupid crap imaginable because if you
    want to
See God and have God see you and have this mutual
    perception
Be completely untrammeled by blather and greed and
    comment,
Go stand in the street as the kindergarten bus murmurs
    past. I'm

Not kidding and this is not a metaphor. I am completely
    serious.
Everyone babbles about God but I saw God this
    morning just as
The bus slowed down for the stop on Maple Street. God
    was six
Girls and one boy with a bright green and purple
    stegosaurus hat.
Of course God would wear a brilliantly colored tall
    dinosaur hat!
If you were the Imagination that dreamed up everything
    that ever
Was in this blistering perfect terrible world, wouldn't you
    wear a
Hat celebrating some of the wildest most amazing
    developments?

34

God Owns a Convenience Store in British Columbia— Who Knew?

Gae Rusk

God owns a convenience store in the city of Vancouver, in Canada. His store is on Broadway, not far from the University, and God sells everything there, lottery tickets, pastries, beer, paper towels, but what I need is cash, so I park and go in to use the store's convenient money machine, from which I happily buy two hundred Canadian dollars.

In this incarnation, God made himself into a man from North India, running a small business in Canada. This time, God made me into a woman from Oklahoma, raised in New Mexico.

I look up from the money machine and see God standing behind the counter watching me.

After counting my new cash, I am impelled to buy something to legitimize my use of the money machine, but what? Not fruit pies. Not fancy air fresheners, not arthritis-repelling bracelets, but what? I circle the aisles, passing cases of chilled beverages and racks of salted chips. Then I find a candy display bulwarking the cash register at the heart of the store. I love candy, and I love that God sells candy, and I am thinking this very thought when I spy pink grapefruit Mentos.

I first heard about this new flavor from another Mento junkie who bought a roll in Tokyo, and I have suffered Mento envy ever since. Now, glory be to God, here are pink grapefruit Mentos for sale in His crowded convenience store on Broadway.

I pull out twenty dollars, still warm from the money machine, to pay for four rolls of Mentos. I want all the rolls, all thirty or more, but I cannot practice such greed right in front of God, nor can I lie and claim the candy is for my son's soccer team, so I plunk down the money next to those mere four rolls of Mentos, and it is at this moment that God grabs my hand and studies my rings.

They are reddish-purple stars, either rubies or sapphires, depending on the light and whom you believe. One is set in gold, I had it made in Katmandu many years ago, and my older daughter gave me the other one, the one set in silver. I wear both rings twined together to remind me that I am wed to my children and wed to myself, and it is up to me to make it all work for everyone.

God brushes the Mentos aside and touches my wrist. I worry the candy will roll away, but it doesn't budge and instead sits there sparkling and humming. God studies my two rings. He peers into my palm. He asks my birth date. God forgot my birthday? He must be getting old, too.

God's hands are rough and dry, the hands of someone who works for a living. They are perfectly warm. They vibrate. His eyes are mirrors of mica and mercury. His eyes compel me to listen. They adjure me to remember what He says as He reads my palms like the lyrics of two hymns in a key I have never before heard.

When God works out my numerology on a sales slip, the results make him smile. He tells me many true things right there at the checkout counter, then he works the numbers for my three kids, for my parents, for my ex-husband, even for my first boyfriend, and I am transfixed by it all.

When I have to leave, God leans forward and tells me I have a big angel living in my heart. Huge, he says. Enormous. According to God, at least half my heart is filled with this lively angel, who irradiates my blood and drives my deeds and generally lights the runway of life for me, and for anyone else who lands nearby.

God finally releases my hands. I look at them to see if the pulsing sensation is visible. My hands look normal, except the two rubies are strobing brilliant stars. God blesses me as I stumble off, my stunned hands clutching four rolls of Mentos in the prayer position. God warns me to drive more carefully. He says he has noticed my tendency to be other-minded, and I marvel again that He knows me so well.

Then I drive more erratically than ever, because my angel is wide-awake and throbbing in my chest, my rings are blinding the oncoming traffic, and it is hard to hold the wheel with my hands still needling back to normal.

Love Notes

The joyful experience of being loved by God makes it impossible for us to separate loving God from loving others. No matter how we express our love for one another, we may be sure that God will multiply His Presence to us. For we are nearest God when we love.

—SUE MONK KIDD,
GOD'S JOYFUL SURPRISE

I am grateful to have been loved and to be loved now and to be able to love, because that liberates. Love liberates. It doesn't just hold—that's ego. Love liberates. It doesn't bind. Love says, I love you. I love you if you're in China. I love you if you're across town. I love you if you're in Harlem. I love you. I would like to be near you. I'd like to have your arms around me. I'd like to

hear your voice in my ear. But that's
not possible now, so I love you. Go.

—Maya Angelou

The mystery of God's love as I under-
stand it is that God loves the man who
was being mean to his dog just as much
as he loves babies; God loves Susan
Smith, who drowned her two sons, as
much as he loves Desmond Tutu. And
he loved her just as much when she
was releasing the handbrake of her car
that sent her boys into the river as he
did when she first nursed them. So of
course, he loves old ordinary me, even
or especially at my most scared and
petty and mean and obsessive. Loves
me; chooses me.

—Anne Lamott,
Traveling Mercies

The prayer of beholding endeavors to
see spiritually in the mind's eye what
really is beneath what seems to be.
Someone may be a very aggressive,
cruel, and objectionable character, but
beneath that we know that he is a child

of God. The important differentiation is that there must be no thought of what should be. We seek to behold what really is.

—THOMAS HORA

We honor the preciousness of people and see the face of God in them all.

—VINCENT DE PAUL

The Parable of the Prodigal Son

Luke 15:11–32

Then Jesus said, "There was a man who had two sons. The younger of them said to his father, 'Father, give me the share of the property that will belong to me.' So he divided his property between them. A few days later the younger son gathered all he had and traveled to a distant country, and there he squandered his property in dissolute living. When he had spent everything, a severe famine took place throughout that country, and he began to be in need. So he went and hired himself out to one of the citizens of that country, who sent him to his fields to feed the pigs. He would gladly have filled himself with the pods that the pigs were eating; and no one gave him anything.

"But when he came to himself he said, 'How many of my father's hired hands have bread enough and to spare, but here I am dying of hunger! I will get up and go to my father, and I will say to him, "Father, I have sinned against heaven and before you; I am no longer worthy to be called your son; treat me like one of your hired hands."' So he set off and went to his father. But while he was still far off, his father saw him and was filled with compassion; he ran and put his arms around him and kissed him.

"Then the son said to him, 'Father, I have sinned against heaven and before you; I am no longer worthy to be called your son.'

"But the father said to his slaves, 'Quickly, bring out a robe—the best one—and put it on him; put a ring on his finger and sandals on his feet. And get the fatted calf and kill it, and let us eat and celebrate; for this son of mine was dead and is alive again; he was lost and is found!'

"And they began to celebrate."

36

This Tremendous Lover

Dom Eugene Boylan

No matter how great, how numerous, how malicious are our sins, even if we had spent every moment of our life in deliberate mortal sin against God, still one single act of love of God for His own sake can destroy every single sin on our soul; and even if our love be but imperfect, even if our sorrow arises rather from love of ourselves—inasmuch as we deplore our supernatural loss—than from love of Him, still He is waiting for us in the sacrament of penance, to forgive us and to change our imperfect sorrow into love of Him, making us His friend by grace. No sins in our past of which we are willing to repent are any barrier to our reaching the summits of sanctity.

The reason is because our sanctification is from God and from His mercy. Listen to our Lord's words on the night He was betrayed: "For them do I sanctify myself, that they also may be sanctified in truth"; and consider St. Augustine's explanation of His meaning.

What else can He mean but this: "I sanctify them myself, since they are truly myself." For they of whom He speaks are His members, and the head and body are one Christ. . . . That He signifies this unity is certain from the remainder of the same verse. For having said: "For them do I sanctify myself," He immediately adds: "In order that they too may be sanctified in truth," to show that He refers to the holiness that we are to receive from Him. Now the words "in truth" can only mean "in me," since Truth is the Word who in the beginning was God. . . . "And for them do I sanctify myself," that is "I sanctify them in myself as myself, since in me they too are myself." "In order that they may be sanctified as I am sanctified," that is to say "in truth which is I myself."

Quia et ipsi sunt ego: "since they too are myself"! That is why no one who is willing to love God is prevented from reaching the heights of holiness and all that is essentially connected with it. Because if anyone is willing to love God—and by that very fact one does love Him—our Lord can say of him, "he too is myself"; and He has sanctified him in Himself and has already won the holiness that such a one is to receive from Him. By truly loving Christ we become members of Christ, and if we do His will by keeping His commandments, the Father and He will come and make Their abode in us.

The whole Christian life, then, is Christ and His love. We ourselves live and love no longer, it is Christ who lives and loves in us. In Christ we are loved, and Christ is loved in us. In us Christ loves the Father, and the Father loves Christ in us. Christ in us loves our neighbor, and in our neighbor we love Christ. Christ in the husband loves the wife, and in the wife the husband loves Christ. So also Christ in the wife loves the husband, and in the husband the wife loves Christ. Christ is our supplement, our complement, our All in fact, both in loving and being loved, "And there shall be one Christ loving Himself." For "Christ is all and in all" (Col 3:11).

37

Don't Give Up on God, or Yourself

Josephine Robertson

Don't give up on God, or yourself, or the mysteries buried among the roots of trees, standings stones, and cathedral bones. If you were not introduced to a God worthy of love as a child you can still meet her now. As I grew too old for hiding under altars and spending evenings curled up in my Mother's lap I met other wild-eyed souls who introduced me to a more grown up sort of Love.

There was Rumi, constantly drunk on the wine of Creation. And Hafiz spinning sonnets of pure bliss for the immortal Beloved. Mary Oliver, John O'Donohue, Madeleine L'Engle, Julian, Brigit, and Hildegard to name a few. Their words and their love march on and on into time overflowing with the sweet red wine of mysticism. Christian, Jewish, Muslim, and more.

What unites us is that wild, soul stirring longing for One beyond all names. But who we are constantly describing.

Somehow, in the midst of crappy theology and religious politics our great religious traditions have somehow fostered mystics, poets, and other creative souls. I trust that the Divine is still alive and well even in our human institutions simply because they still produce such people, even as they fail at much else.

If your religious fare has been repression, anger, and a vindictive God out to get you (but of course called loving) a deep dive into the mystics, the poets, the dreamers of the religious world (of any faith tradition!) can feel like a dive into a cool refreshing body of water. Buoyant, cleansing, strange, and new. (Come in, the water is fine!)

The Divine is already madly in love with you, head over heels, giddy. It was love at first sight for Them. You might not believe it, but She took one look at you and that was it, He was hopelessly in love. Always has been, always will be. We don't hear this enough. How much easier to fall madly in love when you know you are already loved, madly?

And here is what I love so much about the Divine. She isn't pushy. She's loved me from before time, but she won't rush me into anything. She does not force herself on me. She waits in quiet still places, in the dark, the stars, the lilies. Oh sure, she puts herself out there, flashy, in every over designed snowflake, in constellations filled in with stars we cannot even see (their light hasn't had time to arrive, give it a millennia). But she doesn't *demand* anything in return.

You can feast on her beauty your whole life long and she will never be less generous because you gave nothing back. (Oh but They will miss you.) There is no manipulation, no guilt, no coercion in the Divine. There is gift, and invitation, and waiting. For you. But if you never knock on her door, if you never do more than enjoy the gifts she has given there will be no stormy letter in your mailbox, no guilt inducing phone call.

(But I think you will be missing something.)

If you fall in love with God, it will be because you let go and let yourself fall. God will not push you, or drag you down.

But she will always be waiting, ready, excited to catch you, you beautiful comet.

That We May Love
as You Love!

Unknown

Bless us with Love, O Merciful God;
That we may Love as you Love!
That we may show patience, tolerance,
Kindness, caring, and love to all!
Give me knowledge, O giver of Knowledge,
That I may be one with my Universe and Mother Earth!
O Compassionate One, grant compassion unto us;
That we may help all fellow souls in need!
Bless us with your Love, O God.
Bless us with your Love.

"I Am Wherever There Is Love"

Joy Scrivener

Our 14-year-old dog Abbey died last month. The day after she passed away my 4-year-old daughter Meredith was crying and talking about how much she missed Abbey. She asked if we could write a letter to God so that when Abbey got to heaven, God would recognize her. I told her that I thought we could do so, and she dictated these words:

> *Dear God,*
>
> *Will you please take care of my dog? She died yesterday and is with you in heaven. I miss her very much. I am happy that you let me have her as my dog even though she got sick. I hope you will play with her. She likes to swim and play with balls. I am sending a picture of her so when you see*

*her you will know that she is my dog. I
really miss her.*

Love, Meredith

We put the letter in an envelope with a picture of Abbey
and Meredith and addressed it to God/Heaven. We put our
return address on it. Then Meredith pasted several stamps
on the front of the envelope because she said it would take
lots of stamps to get the letter all the way to heaven. That
afternoon she dropped it into the letterbox at the post office. A few days later, she asked if God had gotten the letter
yet. I told her that I thought He had.

Yesterday, there was a package wrapped in gold paper on
our front porch addressed, "To Meredith" in an unfamiliar
hand. Meredith opened it. Inside was a book by Mr. Rogers called, "When a Pet Dies." Taped to the inside front
cover was the letter we had written to God in its opened
envelope. On the opposite page were the picture of Abbey
& Meredith and this note:

> *Dear Meredith,*
>
> *Abbey arrived safely in heaven.
> Having the picture was a big help
> and I recognized her right away.
> Abbey isn't sick anymore. Her spirit is
> here with me just like it stays in your
> heart. Abbey loved being your dog. Since
> we don't need our bodies in heaven, I*

don't have any pockets to keep your picture in so I am sending it back to you in this little book for you to keep and have something to remember Abbey by. Thank you for the beautiful letter and thank your mother for helping you write it and sending it to me. What a wonderful mother you have. I picked her especially for you. I send my blessings every day and remember that I love you very much. By the way, I'm easy to find. I am wherever there is love.

Love, God

Love Notes

If you want to know God,
become love. If you want
to know others, become love.
If you want to know yourself,
become love. And if you want
to know love, forget all you
thought you knew or needed
to know, and become love.

—Meister Eckhart

He who is filled with love is filled with
God himself.

—St. Augustine

PART THREE

LOVE OF NEIGHBOR

If I love myself, I love you.
If I love you, I love myself.

—RUMI

40

The Parable of the Good Samaritan

Luke 10:25–37

Then a teacher of the Law came and began putting Jesus to the test. And he said, "Master, what shall I do to receive eternal life?"

Jesus replied, "What is written in the Scripture? How do you understand it?"

The man answered, "It is written: You shall love the Lord God with all your heart, with all your soul, with all your strength and with all your mind. And you shall love your neighbor as yourself."

Jesus replied, "What a good answer!" Do this and you shall live."

The man wanted to keep up appearances, so he replied, "Who is my neighbor?"

Jesus then said, "There was a man going down from Jerusalem to Jericho and he fell into the hands of robbers. They stripped him, beat him and went off leaving him half-dead. It happened that a priest was going along that road and saw the man, but passed by on the other side. Likewise, a Levite saw the man and passed by on the other side. But a Samaritan, too, was going that way, and when he came upon the man, he was moved with compassion. He went over to him and treated his wounds with oil and wine and wrapped them with bandages. Then he put him on his own mount and brought him to an inn where he took care of him. . . . Jesus then asked, "Which of these three, do you think, made himself neighbor to the man who fell in the hands of robbers?"

The teacher of the Law answered, "The one who had mercy on him."

And Jesus said, "Go then and do the same."

Who Is My Neighbor?

Frederic Buechner

When Jesus said to love your neighbor, a lawyer who was present asked him to clarify what he meant by neighbor. He wanted a legal definition he could refer to in case the question of loving one ever happened to come up. He presumably wanted something on the order of: "A neighbor (hereinafter referred to as the party of the first part) is to be construed as meaning a person of Jewish descent whose legal residence is within a radius of no more than three statute miles from one's own legal residence unless there is another person of Jewish descent (hereinafter to be referred to as the party of the second part) living closer to the party of the first part than one is oneself, in which case the party of the second part is to be construed as neighbor to the party of the first part and one is oneself relieved of all responsibility of any sort or kind whatsoever." Instead, Jesus told the story of the Good Samaritan (Luke 10:25–37), the point of which seems to be that your neighbor is to be construed as meaning anybody who needs you. The lawyer's response is left unrecorded.

Love Your Neighbor

Cynthia Bourgeault

When Jesus talks about Oneness, he is not speaking in an Eastern sense about an equivalency of being, such that I am in and of myself divine. Rather, what he has in mind is a complete, mutual indwelling: I am in God, God is in you, you are in God, we are in each other.

His most beautiful symbol for this is in John 15 where he says, "I am the vine; you are the branches. Abide in me as I in you" (15:4–5). A few verses later he says, "As the Father has loved me, so I have loved you. Abide in my love" (15:9). While he does indeed claim that "the Father and I are one" (John 10:30)—a statement so blasphemous to Jewish ears that it nearly gets Jesus stoned—he does not see this as an exclusive privilege but as something shared by all human beings. There is no separation between humans and God because of this mutual inter-abiding which expresses the indivisible reality of divine love.

We flow into God—and God into us—because it is the nature of love to flow. And as we give ourselves into one another in this fashion, the vine gives life and coherence to the branch while the branch makes visible what the vine is. (After all, a vine is merely an abstraction until there are actual branches to articulate its reality.) The whole and the part live together in mutual, loving reciprocity, each belonging to the other and dependent on the other to show forth the fullness of love. That's Jesus' vision of no separation between human and Divine.

No separation between human and human is an equally powerful notion—and equally challenging. One of the most familiar of Jesus' teachings is "Love your neighbor as yourself" (Mark 12:31, Matthew 22:39). But we almost always hear that wrong: "Love your neighbor as much as yourself." (And of course, the next logical question then becomes, "But I have to love me first, don't I, before I can love my neighbor?") If you listen closely to Jesus however, there is no "as much as" in his admonition. It's just "Love your neighbor as yourself"—as a continuation of your very own being. It's a complete seeing that your neighbor is you. There are not two individuals out there, one seeking to better herself at the price of the other, or to extend charity to the other; there are simply two cells of the one great Life. Each of them is equally precious and necessary. And as these two cells flow into one another, experiencing that one Life from the inside, they discover that "laying down one's life for another" is not a loss of one's self but a vast expansion of it—because the indivisible reality of love is the only True Self.

43

Love Whatever Arises

Matt Kahn

Instead of trying to silence your mind chatter,
simply love the one who wants to chat.
Instead of trying to shift your feelings,
just love the one who can't stop feeling.
Instead of trying to resolve each fear,
simply love the one who's always afraid.
Instead of trying to not take things personally,
just love the one came here to make life personal.
Instead of trying to prove your worth,
simply love the one who feels worthless, lost, ashamed,
and alone.
Instead of trying to leap forward in evolution,
just love the one who feels left behind.
Instead of having something to prove,
simply love the one who came here to play.
Instead of bossing yourself around and measuring
your progress through spiritual obedience,
 just love the one who refuses to listen.

Matt Kahn

Instead of trying to believe,
simply love the one in doubt.
Instead of trying whatever you attempt,
just love the one who needs permission to be.
Whatever arises, love that.
This is the way of an awakening heart.

44

Love from Neighbors on the Margins

Edwina Gateley

On the margins one encounters people who are truly dependent on God and on each other. Late one night I did not have to venture far to encounter such a reality. Walking down a busy street, I was passing a huge old church. Parked at the bottom of its worn concrete steps were three shopping carts piled high with plastic bags full of trophies and bits of junk collected from the streets and the dumpsters. Five elderly homeless women (known as shopping bag ladies) had arranged themselves on the church steps—one at the top and two on each edge of the next two steps going downward. In the center they had placed a large plastic bottle of ginger ale surrounded by some cookies (smuggled, no doubt, from the nearby soup kitchen) and some styrofoam cups from McDonalds. It was almost midnight. I hesitated and looked up at the unlikely gathering.

"We're having a picnic," yelled one of the women above the sound of a passing car. "Come and join us!" I joined them. Sitting on the bottom step I was given a napkin and a cup of ginger ale, then a cookie was decorously passed from hand to hand toward me. It had traveled far—like the ladies themselves.

Night fell. Gradually the ladies ceased to chatter and to laugh. The traffic thinned. We all knew it was time to sleep. Along with the silence, a deep, deep loneliness fell upon our little party. And in me arose a deep shame for the rich country in which I lived, a country that could not share its multiple resources with the very poor even as these very poor shared with me the little they had. How much more clearly the poor can live in solidarity and give us a vision of a new way of being. They had not hesitated to invite me to their party; their fare was meager, but their hearts—broken open—were large enough to invite me in. There was magic on the margins that cold, damp night. Through the homeless women who shared their midnight picnic with me, I myself was drawn into the ranks of the marginalized. For to choose the margins leaves one in a different place than before. One's own social identity shifts and changes as one experiences and becomes part of a new and transforming reality. That reality is compassion. True compassion is not about being at one with one's own social cultural group, but it is being able to see and know oneself as connected to every person without reservation. The words of Jesus, "I am in you and you are in me," became gloriously real and alive on society's edges. That experience itself is the magic of the margins.

45

When You Thought
I Wasn't Looking

Mary Rita Schilke Sill

Inspired by my mother,
Blanche Elizabeth Montgomery.

When you thought I wasn't looking
You hung my first painting on the refrigerator
And I wanted to paint another.

When you thought I wasn't looking
You fed a stray cat
And I thought it was good to be kind to animals.

When you thought I wasn't looking
You baked a birthday cake just for me
And I knew that little things were special things.

When you thought I wasn't looking

You said a prayer
And I believed there was a God that I could always talk to.

When you thought I wasn't looking
You kissed me goodnight
And I felt loved.

When you thought I wasn't looking
I saw tears come from your eyes
And I learned that sometimes things hurt
But that it's all right to cry.

When you thought I wasn't looking
You smiled
And it made me want to look that pretty too.

When you thought I wasn't looking
You cared
And I wanted to be everything I could be.

When you thought I wasn't looking
I looked
And I wanted to say thanks
For all the things you did
When you thought I wasn't looking.

46

Loving-Kindness: Blessing Your Corner of the World with Love

Victor Parachin

> *Put away all hindrances, let your mind*
> *full of love pervade . . . the whole wide*
> *world, above, below, around and every-*
> *where, altogether continue to pervade*
> *with love-filled thought, abounding,*
> *sublime, beyond measure.*
>
> —THE BUDDHA

In every authentic spiritual life there is the quality of loving-kindness. While this can arise naturally in some circumstances, such as the love of a parent for a child or a partner for a spouse, on most other occasions it must be intentionally cultivated. One ancient practice (it goes back at least twenty-five hundred years) is the loving-kindness meditation. It is easy to do and highly satisfying because it evokes friendliness and compassion toward oneself and toward others.

To begin, find a quiet place where you can repeat to yourself the simple words of this meditation. It can be done in your home, office, or car; in a park, on a playground; on buses or airplanes; in doctors' waiting rooms—anywhere you can sit comfortably and be quiet. If you're new to meditation practices, try doing this for a mere five minutes. If you've had a little more experience or have a little more time, try spending ten to twenty minutes on it. This loving-kindness meditation begins with yourself and then radiates outward. It is recommended that we start with the self because it is difficult to love others if we are unable to love ourselves.

Begin by placing the focus on yourself, and then repeat these four sentences:

> *May I be filled with loving-kindness.*
> *May I be free of suffering.*
> *May I be at peace.*
> *May I be happy.*

Repeat the four sentences, allowing their good intentions to sink deeply into your body and mind.

Then place the focus on someone you love:

> *May (name) be filled with loving-kindness.*
> *May (name) be free of suffering.*
> *May (name) be at peace.*
> *May (name) be happy.*

Again, repeat these so that you will evoke loving-kindness toward your loved one.

Next, offer this meditation for a friend or colleague:

> *May (name) be filled with loving-kindness.*
> *May (name) be free of suffering.*
> *May (name) be at peace.*
> *May (name) be happy.*

Repeat the four sentences to deepen loving-kindness attitudes toward this person.

On the next cycle, offer the meditation for a stranger, perhaps the man who makes your coffee at your favorite coffee shop, or the woman who rides the same bus as you do:

> *May he/she be filled with loving-kindness.*
> *May he/she be free of suffering.*
> *May he/she be at peace.*
> *May he/she be happy.*

As you continue to repeat these, you will begin to feel a sense of compassion toward these strangers who are part of your life.

Finally, if you really want to challenge yourself, offer the loving-kindness meditation for an enemy or some difficult person in your life. It may be someone who has treated you unkindly or even cruelly, or someone who betrayed your confidence. Perhaps it may be someone who has gossiped about you and hurt you deeply:

> *May (name) be filled with loving-kindness.*
> *May (name) be free of suffering.*
> *May (name) be at peace.*
> *May (name) be happy.*

Continue repeating until your feelings of anger, hurt, and disappointment begin to soften. Most people discover that this loving-kindness meditation is calming and enlarges the heart.

Love Notes

Dear friends, let us love each other,
because love is from God, and everyone
who loves is born from God and knows
God. The person who doesn't love does
not know God, because God is love.

—1 JOHN 4:7–8

One who lives in God lives in others
because it is in the other that God is
found.

—ILIA DELIO

Do not waste time bothering whether you
"love" your neighbor; act as if you did.
As soon as we do this, we find one of
the great secrets. When you are behav-
ing as if you loved someone, you will
presently come to love him.

—C. S. LEWIS

Love Notes

*A purpose of human life, no matter
who is controlling it, is to love whoever
is around to be loved.*

—KURT VONNEGUT JR.

*If you must love your neighbor as your-
self, it is at least as fair to love yourself
as your neighbor.*

—NICOLAS CHAMFORT

47

Love Your Enemies

Matthew and Luke

You have heard that it was said: An eye for an eye and a tooth for a tooth. But I tell you this: do not oppose evil with evil; if someone slaps you on your right cheek, turn and offer the other. If someone sues you in court for your shirt, give your coat as well. If someone forces you to go one mile, go also the second mile. Give when asked and do not turn your back on anyone who wants to borrow from you.

You have heard that it was said: Love your neighbor and do not do good to your enemy. But this I tell you: Love your enemies, and pray for those who persecute you, so that you may be children of your Father in Heaven. For he makes his sun rise on both the wicked and the good.

—MATTHEW 5:38–45

Love your enemies, do good to those who hate you. Bless those who curse you and pray for those who treat you badly. To the one who strikes you on the cheek, turn the other cheek; from the one who takes your coat, do not keep back your shirt. Give to the one who asks and if anyone has taken something from you, do not demand it back. Do to others as you would have others do to you. If you love only those who love you, what kind of graciousness is yours? Even sinners love those who love them. If you do favors to those who are good to you, what kind of graciousness is yours? Even sinners do the same. If you lend only when you expect to receive, what kind of graciousness is yours? For sinners also lend to sinners, expecting to receive something in return. But love your enemies and do good to them, and lend when there is nothing to expect in return. Then will your reward be great and you will be sons and daughters of the Most High. For He is kind towards the ungrateful and the wicked.

Be merciful, just as your Father is merciful.

—Luke 6:27–36

48

We Love Each Other That's Enough

Ram Dass and Paul Gorman

God bless my mother, and God bless me. We made it through.

She had a stroke and long period of rehabilitation, and it was clear she was going to have to stay with us for a while. I had all these things in mind: it was a chance to pay her back for all those years. There were these things I was going help her clear up, like the way she was thinking. I wanted to do the whole job very well, this big opportunity. We should all feel good about it at the end. Little things like that. Some "little"!

Fights? Classics, like only a mother and daughter can have. And my mother is a great fighter, from the Old School of somehow loving it and being very good at it and getting a kind of ecstatic look in your eye when you're really into it. I guess I'm exaggerating. It drives me a little crazy. I hate to argue. Oh, well. . . .

But it got bad. Over a hard-boiled egg we had a bad fight. We'd both gotten worn out, irritable, and frustrated. Boom! I don't remember what about—just about how it was all going and why her stay had gotten difficult and all of us had become more and more irritable and short-tempered.

In the middle of it, she stopped short and said, "Why are you doing all this for me anyway?" It sort of hit me and I started to list all the reasons. They just came out: I was afraid for her; I wanted to get her well; I felt maybe I'd ignored her when I was younger; I needed to show her I was strong; I needed to get her ready for going home alone; old age; and on and on. I was amazed myself. I could have gone on giving reasons all night. Even she was impressed.

"Junk," she said when I was done.

"Junk?" I yelled. Like, boy, she'd made a real mistake with that remark. I could really get her.

"Yes, junk," she said again, but a little more quietly. And that little-more-quietly tone got me. And she went on: "You don't have to have all those reasons. We love each other. That's enough."

I felt like a child again. Having your parents show you something that's true, but you don't feel put down—you feel better, because it is true, and you know it, even though you are a child. I said, "You're right. You're really right. I'm sorry." She said, "Don't be sorry. Junk is fine. It's what you don't need anymore. I love you."

It was a wonderful moment, and the fight stopped, which my mother accepted a little reluctantly. No, I'm joking—she was very pleased. She saw how it all was. Everything after that was just, well, easier—less pressure, less trying, less pushing, happening more by itself. And the visit ended up fine. We just spent time together, and then she went back to her house.

~

49

Save Your Best
for Someone Else

Donna Ashworth

Dear Friend,

I don't need you at your best when you come to my home.

I don't care what you are wearing or what car you drove here.

I don't care if there is food on your shirt and your hair is full of knots.

None of that matters to me.

I care about you.

I care about what's in your heart, how afraid you are. What you worry about in the night.

I care about your deepest fears and your biggest dreams and I am there for it all.

If you mess up, I won't judge.

That's my promise to you.

So, don't cancel me because your house is a mess and your cupboards are bare.

I will bring what you need with pleasure and I will listen to your problems without measure or malice. If you are on the floor, I'm picking you up, or I'm sitting down beside you.

You need never be alone down there.

And before I leave, I will have made you smile at least once.

That's my promise to you.

So, save your best for someone else my friend because I want you just as you are.

That's what friends are for.

50

Love at Its Best

John Lewis

I think sometimes people are afraid to say I love you. Especially in public life, many elected officials or worldly elected officials are afraid to talk about love. Maybe people tend to think something is so emotional about it. Maybe it's a sign of weakness. And we're not supposed to cry. We're supposed to be strong, but love is strong. Love is powerful.

The movement created what I like to call a nonviolent revolution. It was love at its best. It's one of the highest forms of love. That you beat me, you arrest me, you take me to jail, you almost kill me, but in spite of that, I'm going to still love you. I know Dr. King used to joke sometime and say things like, "Just love the hell outta everybody. Just love 'em."

Love Notes

I beg you, look for the words "social justice" or "economic justice" on your church website. If you find it, run as fast as you can. Social justice and economic justice, they are code words. Now, am I advising people to leave their church? Yes!

—GLENN BECK

All the believers were united in heart and mind. And they felt that what they owned was not their own, so they shared everything they had. The apostles testified powerfully to the resurrection of the Lord Jesus, and God's great blessing was upon them all. There were no needy people among them, because those who owned land or houses would sell them and bring the money

146

to the apostles to distribute to anyone
according to their need.

—ACTS 4:32–35

The difference between communism
and Christianity? Communism says
you must be good. Christianity says it's
good to be good.

Love of neighbor, says every religion,
has a communal as well as individual
dimension, a justice aspect as well as a
mercy one.

So if you see the words "social
justice" or "economic justice" on a sign
in front of your church or synagogue
or mosque, you can know they are not
codes for communism but symbols of the
love of being loving.

—MICHAEL LEACH

Why Are You Here?

Vincent P. Cole

It was early morning on my first day in Irian Jaya. I was trying to get settled in my new home when an old Asmat fellow walked in without knocking and made himself comfortable in one of the chairs.

My previous experience in Indonesia taught me never to go straight to the point with people. We talked a long time, but when the old gentleman gave me no clues as to why he had come, I went back to my work, figuring he would catch on and disappear. He didn't.

I felt uncomfortable having him sitting there, so I came back and blurted out, "Is there something you want?" "No," he answered as he calmly stretched himself out on the short couch. Mildly irritated I said, "Hey, look, if you don't want anything, why are you here?" This ex-headhunter, who was to become one of my dearest friends and mentors, looked puzzled and replied simply, "Because you are alone."

Stand Up for the Stupid and Crazy

Walt Whitman

This is what you shall do; Love the earth and sun and the animals, despise riches, give alms to everyone that asks, stand up for the stupid and crazy, devote your income and labor to others, hate tyrants, argue not concerning God, have patience and indulgence toward the people, take off your hat to nothing known or unknown or to any man or number of men, go freely with powerful uneducated persons and with the young and with the mothers of families, read these leaves in the open air every season of every year of your life, re-examine all you have been told at school or church or in any book, dismiss whatever insults your own soul, and your very flesh shall be a great poem and have the richest fluency not only in its words but in the silent lines of its lips and face and between the lashes of your eyes and in every motion and joint of your body.

Love Deeply

Henri J. M. Nouwen

Do not hesitate to love and to love deeply.

You might be afraid of the pain that deep love can cause. When those you love deeply reject you, leave you, or die, your heart will be broken. But that should not hold you back from loving deeply. The pain that comes from deep love makes your love ever more fruitful. It is like a plow that breaks the ground to allow the seed to take root and grow into a strong plant. Every time you experience the pain of rejection, absence, or death, you are faced with a choice. You can become bitter and decide not to love again, or you can stand straight in your pain and let the soil on which you stand become richer and more able to give life to new seeds.

The more you have loved and have allowed yourself to suffer because of your love, the more you will be able to let your heart grow wider and deeper. When your love is truly giving and receiving, those whom you love will not leave your heart even when they depart from you. They will become part of yourself and thus gradually build a community within you.

Those you have deeply loved become part of you. The longer you live, there will always be more people to be loved by you and to become part of your inner community. The wider your inner community becomes, the more easily you will recognize your own brothers and sisters in the strangers around you. Those who are alive within you will recognize those who are alive around you. The wider the community of your heart, the wider the community around you. Thus the pain of rejection, absence, and death can become fruitful. Yes, as you love deeply the ground of your heart will be broken more and more, but you will rejoice in the abundance of the fruit it will bear.

Love Notes

Love your enemies. That is the hardest saying of all. Please, Father in heaven who made me, take away my heart of stone and give me a heart of flesh to love my enemy. It is a terrible thought—"we love God as much as the one we love the least."

—Dorothy Day

Forgive everyone who hurts you. They are suffering already. You are loved beyond anything you can currently perceive. Be brave and do not fall asleep.

—Donna Goddard

Men think that it is impossible for a human being to love his enemies, for enemies are hardly able to endure the sight of one another. Well, then, shut

Love Notes

your eyes—and your enemy looks just
like your neighbor.

—Søren Kierkegaard

The toughest thing is to love somebody
who has done something mean to you.
Especially when that somebody has
been yourself.

—Mr. Rogers

54

A Piece of Light

Joyce Rupp

*As the sun rose, it filled me until I
thought I was all light and there was
nothing left of what I once called ME.
Then suddenly I saw below at the
water's edge another sister of light. My
light streamed out to her. Her light
flowed back to me and we were one in
the light.*

—Macrina Wiederkehr

There is a piece of light in all of us,
easily seen in the wise Thomas Berry
longing to heal the wounds of our planet,
in Dorothy Day who embraced the poor,
and Mahatma Gandhi, fighting for peace
with the weapon of nonviolence.

Joyce Rupp

There is a piece of light in all of us,
the grandmothers and grandfathers,
children orphaned by AIDS and war,
the feeble, the lame, the disheartened,
the successful as well as the searcher.

There is a piece of light in all of us,
maybe hidden or buried with pain,
perhaps pushed in the corner by shame.
It is there in the arrogant, the hateful,
racists, torturers, and abusers,
and ones who are willing to kill.

Seen or unseen, the light is there,
ready to kindle, eager to expand,
refusing to be tightly contained.
As soon as the tiniest space is allowed
it quickly emerges, floods outward,
illuminating the darkest of places.

One single candle lights a little dark space.
Many candles light a world full of people
desperately in need of each other's glow.
Each lone light makes us stronger
when we all stand together.

55

Tend to What Repulses You

Pauline Hovey

"Tend to what repulses you."

This is what I "hear" in my morning meditation. I had been reflecting on Jesus washing his disciples' feet—a scene so vivid in my imagination—foul-smelling, calloused, bare feet waiting for their turn to be bathed. Closing my eyes, I intended to practice *lectio divina*, with whatever word or phrase came to me from the reading. Instead, I was given this phrase, seemingly out of nowhere. *"Tend to what repulses you."*

I don't have to ask for an explanation. The revolting scent of what Jesus encounters captures my senses like never before. Because of what I have experienced in El Paso.

And, yes, it repulses me.

Not unlike the memory of a little boy's dusty feet. A boy no more than 4 years old, his badly worn shoes were covered in a film of dirt from the desert.

Several months earlier, before the so-called "Migrant Protection Protocol" was forcing refugees to wait in dangerous countries, I had assisted Andree, along with his Guatemalan father, in our *roperia*, or clothing room. They had arrived at our temporary hospitality shelter, Casa del Refugiado, earlier that day, dropped off by ICE after being processed and vetted, ready to move on to their family sponsor where they would await their asylum hearing.

As is customary, we provide a change of clothes for all our guests before they take their shower. The El Paso community donates mostly all of the clothing—the rest coming from elsewhere in the country—and usually we have a sufficient supply. But our shoe supply is always minimal. Guests are only allowed to take replacement shoes if their own are falling apart, which this boy's clearly were.

So, when Andree smiled up at me, pointing to the display of children's shoes lined up on the shelf and asked for *zapatos*, I could not deny him. His father sheepishly grinned, already holding in his arms lavish gifts: clean T-shirts and jeans, new underwear and socks—a pair of each for both of them. He felt it was a lot to ask. I knew this without him saying so.

Meekness. Gratefulness. This has been my experience of the Central Americans who have come through our door.

But I told him it was OK and he lifted his son onto a stool, where little Andree's feet were now inches from my face. The color and original shape of his shoes barely recognizable.

Although I did not need to, I chose to help Andree change his shoes. I'd become enamored with this little dark-haired charmer traveling without his mamma, and I wanted to provide a feminine touch that I suspected he might be missing.

Andree giggled as I took his small feet in my palm, teasing him with childish sounds and tickling touches. We both laughed until I removed his filthy shoes. Instinctively, I turned my body away from him.

The stench overpowered me like nothing I'd ever experienced from a child. Including the dirtiest of diapers. I could not have imagined someone's feet being so foul-smelling, much less those of one so small.

To entertain Andree while my senses worked through the shock, I exaggerated disgusting noises and we were soon back to giggling together. I tried not to breathe in too deeply as I slipped another pair of shoes onto his feet.

Later that day, another ICE bus arrived with a new group of migrants, and I joined volunteers to take down the new arrivals' information and connect them with their relatives, their sponsor, who would receive them here in the United States. As I took my place behind the table, I looked out at a sea of people waiting in folding chairs five rows deep. They appeared weary, disheveled, dirty.

A 21-year-old mother sat down before me hoisting a toddler with a runny nose onto her lap. As she answered my questions, I noticed she didn't seem to mind that the phlegm was about to reach her child's lip. I scouted out a tissue from my bag and hurriedly handed it to her. But it was too late. She'd already swiped her shirt sleeve across the little one's nostrils.

I grimaced and moved on to the next question.

Were she and her child traveling alone? Was anyone in their family detained or separated from them during their journey? I assumed the answer was no. Dozens of single mothers with children filled the chairs. Rarely did a couple attempt to get through immigration together nowadays since they'd become aware of the strong possibility of being separated.

But I had to ask. Her answer came through eyes welled with tears.

No longer able to maintain her stoic expression, Stefany cried as she began to relay her story. How the border patrol agents took her husband at the border. How she worried about ever seeing him again. She wondered if she could visit him in detention before heading to his parents, in Virginia, without him.

Another uncomfortable moment. Another instance where I wanted to turn my body away in revulsion. Not let myself feel the anguish in Stefany's eyes. Not feel the pain we are causing so many of these migrants. Simply fill out the paperwork and move on. It would have been so much easier. Instead, I placed my hand over hers. Told her I was sorry this happened. She cried harder.

" . . . *as I have done, so you must do.*"

Yes, Lord, I know you want me to tend to what repulses me. This one day—so clear in my memory—affirms your words.

I know you are asking more of me. More than the symbolic washing of my own son's feet during the Holy Thursday ritual. As special and beautiful as that is, it doesn't challenge me. It doesn't take me out of my circle of safety, down to the floor where the foreign stench from days on distant roads traveled fills my nostrils. Down to the place where another's pain repels me.

Sometimes, to be in service to love goes well beyond being inconvenienced. Sometimes it smells like feet that have been stuffed into shoes worn for weeks on end. Sometimes it is found in the mess and heartbreak of runny noses, bodily odors and disheveled people clasping babies and toddlers, stripped of everything else they'd brought with them. Including their dignity.

Although I may turn from the stench, I will not turn my heart away from tending to what you have placed in front of me. From what you have asked me to do. To follow your example.

No, I cannot turn away.

Don't Look Away

Brené Brown

My mom taught us never to look away from peoples' pain.
The lesson was simple:

> Don't look away, Don't look down,
> Don't pretend not to see hurt.
> Look people in the eye.
> Even when their pain is overwhelming.

> And when you are in pain,
> find the people that can look you in
>   the eye.

We need to know we are not alone, even when we are
hurting.
   This lesson is one of the greatest gifts of my life.

Having Lunch with God

Joseph Healey

A little East African boy in Dar es Salaam wanted to meet God. He knew that it was a long trip to where God lived, so he packed his bag with small, sweet cakes and a large bottle of soda and started on his journey.

He had been on his way for about ten minutes when he met an old woman. She was sitting in a park by the Indian Ocean just staring at some African birds. The boy sat down next to her and opened his bag. He was about to take a drink from his soda when he noticed that the old lady looked hungry, so he offered her a small cake. She gratefully accepted it and smiled at him. Her smile was so pretty that the boy wanted to see it again. So he offered her a drink from his soda. Again she smiled at him. The boy was delighted!

The little East African boy and the old woman sat there all afternoon eating and drinking and smiling, but they never said a word. As it grew dark, the boy realized how tired he was and got up to leave. But before he had gone more than a few steps he turned around, ran back to the old woman and gave her a big hug. She gave him her biggest smile.

When the boy opened the door to his own home a short time later, his mother was surprised by the look of joy on his face.

She asked him, "What did you do today that makes you so happy?"

He replied, "I had lunch with God." But before his mother could respond, he added, "You know what? She's got the most beautiful smile I've ever seen!"

Meanwhile, the old woman, also radiant with joy, returned to her home in the Upanga section of town.

Her son was stunned by the look of peace on her face and he asked, "Mother, what did you do today that makes you so happy?" She replied, "I ate small cakes and drank soda in the park with God." And then, before her son could respond, she added, "You know, he's much younger than I expected."

58

Bishop Morrie Says It's Not about the Soup

Michael Leach

> *Many people are talking about the poor,*
> *but very few people talk to the poor.*
> —Mother Teresa

I eat a sloppy joe in the community kitchen with my classmate Morrie, bishop of Paris, Kansas, then follow him around as he talks with his 36 guests.

Morrie sneaks up behind a little girl sitting at a big round table with her mother and squeezes her shoulders. The girl startles and holds back a smile. "I know who you are, Father!"

"How do you solve a problem like Maria?" Morrie sings badly. "She climbs a tree and scrapes her knee and waltzes on her way to Mass and dooby dooby doo, what are we gonna do?"

"Maybe we give her to you, Padre," says her mother. "She can work for the church and the sisters look after her."

"Noo-oo," Maria says.

"I don't blame you," Morrie says.

"Are you helping out today, Norma?" he asks her mom.

"Sí. I help Jane stock the bookshelves today. Then I go help my lady."

"Norma is a caregiver," Morrie tells me. "She works two jobs, taking care of old people. She volunteers here when she can."

"Father," the girl says, "I bought something today."

"Brought," her mother says. "You brought something today."

"Wonderful. What is it?"

"You won't laugh?"

"Only if you do."

Maria holds up a soft blue blanket. "My blankie," she says. "I don't need it anymore. Someone else can have it."

"She slept with it four years," Norma says. "Never let it go. It makes her feel safe."

"Now it can make someone else safe," Maria says.

"Maria, this is a wonderful gift. May I give you a hug? OK with you, Norma?" Both Maria and Norma get up.

"Do you know that people need three hugs a day just to survive, six to be healthy, and 12 to grow strong? Did I introduce you two to my friend Mike?"

"I know," Norma says as if she's done this gig many times before. "Group hug!"

The four of us group hug, our foreheads touching. "Hold it 10 seconds," Morrie says. "All your stress will disappear."

Ten seconds later, I feel like I had a 10-minute massage.

We bid adieu to Norma and Maria. In the next hour, Morrie spends time with all the guests in the room. He smiles at every one of them. He hugs more than a few and whispers to one of them to call Marge for an appointment to talk about it some more.

My back hurts and I sit down while Morrie continues to work the room. The homeless, those down on their luck, and families just getting by eat together with diocesan staff at tables with white tablecloths and ceramic dishes. The room is as big as a basketball court. Soon after he became bishop of Paris in 1998, Morrie converted this once abandoned meatpacking plant into a Diocesan Center. Most of the building still smells of sheep, but the kitchen is fresher than an empty bottle of Lysol. The two floors above have living quarters, and offices for two priests, three sisters, and seven laypeople who help Morrie run the second smallest diocese in the U.S. He likes to brag that before he got here Paris was the first smallest.

A plaque on the stone wall next to the doorway of the center reads:

> *The bread in your box belongs to the*
> *hungry. The cloak in your closet belongs*
> *to the naked. The shoes you do not*
> *wear belong to the barefoot. The money*
> *in your vault belongs to the destitute.*
>
> —St. Basil the Great

The first-floor kitchen is open five days a week, from 10:30 a.m. to 12:30 p.m. Volunteers cook and serve the meals. The guests are also welcome to take home canned goods or baked bread from the bookshelves along one wall, plus cartons of milk in three packinghouse fridges, and clothes, shoes or toys neatly arranged on folding tables at the far end. The guests, aware of their blessings—and no doubt the words of St. Basil, which is also the name of the tiny basilica on the edge of the prairie—bring goods and gifts themselves whenever they can. That, I guess, is why Maria brought her blankie for someone else to feel safe.

The last guests leave and Morrie pulls up a chair next to mine. "Want a Coke?" he asks.

"No, but you look like you could use one."

"I'm good."

"You know," I tell him. "This is really awesome. Do a lot of dioceses have soup kitchens like this?"

"I like to call it a community kitchen. It's not about the soup."

"I did some research before I flew out here. I read that 50 million Americans, mostly the working poor, have a hard time putting food on the table. Do you think the church could do more?"

"I don't think about that."

We sit in silence for a while. Then Morrie says, "Let's go up to my room for a Coke."

As we lumber by the tables with clothes and shoes and toys, I ask him, "How do you know people won't take stuff they don't need?"

"Honor."

"Does it happen though?"

"It doesn't matter. It's not about the stuff."

"What is it about then?"

Morrie smiles at me.

～

Bishop Morrie is alive and well and living in the imagination of Mike Leach. The Diocese of Paris, Kansas, is located somewhere in his right brain. The Bishop Morrie stories have been a popular feature of Mike's "Soul Seeing" column in the National Catholic Reporter. *You can see them all at https://www.ncronline.org/feature-series/bishop-morrie/stories.*

59

It All Tastes Like Love

Fran Rossi Szpylczyn

Jennie and Darlene are arranging name tags on a folding table in front of the church. "Be my first?" I ask them. Mom and daughter beam. I take my first picture on this special day at the Church of the Immaculate Conception in Glenville, N.Y. I'm Fran, the church office manager.

It's a madcap job, but somebody's got to do it.

I snap a nursing home van as it pulls to the curb. Joan and Pam help old folks in wheelchairs move down the lift as if they were all on a children's ride at the parish carnival. Father Jerry in a white chasuble comes out to greet them. Everyone is as expectant as the biblical Elizabeth when she greeted the young Mary. I click away like Diane Arbus in a sunny mood. The elderly and infirm, along with anyone who wants to be healed, are here to be blessed.

Our twice-yearly anointing Mass will soon begin.

I take a long shot of the Explorers, Jettas and Corollas lined up politely in the parking lot like ambassadors from the United Nations. I snap Rachel, the pastoral care

director and coordinator of the event, as she embraces our
elderly Mary whose coat is as pink as cotton candy. Other
greeters stand at the curb of the church and share hugs and
handshakes and hand out worship aids. My camera captures
the young and the old, the fit and the feeble, the happy and
the weary. I hope the photos will form a collage of one
body of Christ: a portrait of bodies and souls, broken and
whole, immaculately re-conceived and re-membered in this
church on this day. No one will be ignored, left out or cast
aside. The entire body will know that whatever happens to
one of them happens to all of them, and that what happens
to all happens to each.

I blend with the others inside the church and take a picture of the widow Jan who treads up the aisle. Her eyesight
is failing, but she is determined. Helping her into a pew,
I introduce her to Bob and Eileen, a couple who always
manifests cheerfulness despite life's challenges. A photo of
these three will show the beautiful unity in the diversity
of our parish body.

The procession begins. The congregation sings as one:
"Gather us in, the blind and the lame!" Gnarled and shak-
ing hands make the sign of the cross as the liturgy begins.
Everyone listens. We are like children at story time. We
hear scripture passages about healing that assure us of the
promise of Christ.

When it's time for the anointing, Father Jerry approach-
es a row of wheelchairs parked in front of the altar. He
bows, anointing each person with chrism. A man in his 80s

weeps; his aide daubs at his tears with a tissue. I pray that my camera captures the compassion I see with my soul.

Fathers Jerry and Leo move from pew to pew, bearing oil and blessings. Leo anoints Rose, her eyes closed, her up-turned palms extended in a gesture of giving and receiving. Ed is so tall that Jerry must reach up to him. His wife, Ann, is the opposite, and Jerry smiles as he stoops to anoint her.

I put down my camera. Father Jerry's thumb marks a cross on my forehead. When he blesses my palms, the pressure of the crosses traced into each one makes me feel woozy. Without my camera to protect me, I feel vulnerable. I am broken, too. My legs and arms work, my eyes focus, there is no arthritis in my hands, but I need healing, too.

"Go in peace to love and serve the Lord!"

I follow everyone to the parish hall for another kind of banquet. Fran, Anne and other parish nurses have put out a feast of egg, chicken and tuna salad sandwiches. It all tastes like love.

The soundtrack of a community in delight spreads through the room as everyone eats and talks. Father Jerry moves from table to table, leaving a wake of contentment. My camera clicks away as he chats with a spry and playful Clara. Emily who knits us slippers listens in and I photo-graph her, too. Senior citizen George is with Father Leo but he turns his head to smile into my lens like George Clooney as I walk by. I feel like a cameraman in a Fellini movie. The sounds of heaven on Earth fill the room with joyful noise.

We depart greater than when we arrived. We are the body of Christ, broken and restored, dying and rising, reconceived and remembered, here and now, once and forever.

60

A Marriage, an Elegy

Wendell Berry

They lived long, and were faithful
to the good in each other.
They suffered as their faith required.
Now their union is consummate
in earth, and the earth
is their communion. They enter
the serene gravity of the rain,
the hill's passage to the sea.
After long striving, perfect ease.

Love Notes

Nobody escapes being wounded. We are all wounded people, whether physically, emotionally, mentally, or spiritually. The main question is not, "How can we hide our wounds?" so we don't have to be embarrassed, but "How can we put our woundedness in the service of others?" When our wounds cease to be a source of shame, and become a source of healing, we have become wounded healers.

—Henri J. M. Nouwen

It may be only in our own vulnerability, in our actually being wounded, that love gains its full power.

—Gerald May

Love Notes

Do not be dismayed by the brokenness of the world. All things break. And all things can be mended. Not with time, as they say, but with intention. So go. Love intentionally, extravagantly, unconditionally. The broken world waits in darkness for the light that is you.

—L. R. KNOST

Life is fleeting. And if you're ever distressed, cast your eyes to the summer sky when the stars are strung across the velvety night. And when a shooting star streaks through the blackness, turning night into day . . . make a wish and think of me.

—ROBIN WILLIAMS

61

Loving the Christ in Others

Thomas Merton

We have to resolutely put away our attachment to natural appearance and our habit of judging according to the outward face of things. I must learn that my fellow man, just as he is, whether he is my friend or my enemy, my brother or a stranger from the other side of the world . . . "is Christ." . . .

Any prisoner, any starving man, any sick or dying man, any sinner, any man whatever, is to be regarded as Christ—this is the formal command of the Savior Himself. This doctrine is far too simple to satisfy many modern Christians, and undoubtedly many will remain very uneasy with it, tormented by the difficulty that perhaps after all, this particular neighbor is a bad man, and therefore cannot be Christ.

The solution of this difficulty is to unify oneself with the Spirit of Christ, to start thinking and loving as a Christian, and to stop being a hairsplitting pharisee. Our faith is not supposed . . . to assess the state of our neighbor's conscience. It is the needle by which we draw the thread of charity through our neighbor's soul and our own soul and sew ourselves together in one Christ. Our faith is given us not to see whether or not our neighbor is Christ, but to recognize Christ in him and to help our love make both him and ourselves more fully Christ. . . .

Corrupt forms of love wait for the neighbor to "become a worthy object of love" before actually loving him. This is not the way of Christ. Since Christ Himself loved us when we were by no means worthy of love and still loves us with all our unworthiness, our job is to love others without stopping to inquire whether or not they are worthy. . . .

What we are asked to do is to love; and this love itself will render both ourselves and our neighbor worthy if anything can. Indeed, that is one of the most significant things about the power of love. There is no way under the sun to make a man worthy of love except by loving him. As soon as he realizes himself loved—if he is not so weak that he can no longer bear to be loved—he will feel himself instantly becoming worthy of love. He will respond by drawing a mysterious spiritual value out of his own depths, a new identity called into being by the love that is addressed to him.

Christ, Let Me See You in Others

David Adam

Christ, let me see you in others.
Christ, let others see you in me.
Christ, let me see:
You are the caller
you are the poor
you are the stranger at my door.
You are the wanderer
the unfed
you are the homeless
with no bed.
You are the man
driven insane
you are the child
crying in pain.
You are the other who comes to me
open my eyes that I may see.

Christ and Cerebral Palsy

Michael Leach

> *Christ plays in ten thousand places,*
> *lovely in limbs, and lovely in eyes not his,*
> *to the Father through the features of men's faces.*
> —GERARD MANLEY HOPKINS

How easy it is to see the face of Christ in the eyes of a baby or the limbs of a child racing a kite or the features of a movie star. The key to eternal life is to behold the loveliness of Christ in the eyes of a child born blind, the limbs of a teenager with cerebral palsy, the features of a woman scarred with burns. The truth is—the beauty is—each wears the face of Christ and they all play as one.

How many times have I averted my eyes from a picture in *Time* of a starving baby with flies on its face or didn't pay attention to the fellow slumped over in a wheelchair at a wedding or found an excuse not to visit a friend wasting away with cancer or pretended the family at the diner who had a child with Down Syndrome didn't exist? And what a blessing it becomes to begin to see with spiritual eyes and behold the image of the emaciated baby as she really is, *whole*, to touch the cripple in the wheelchair and say hello, to visit a friend or acquaintance in the hospital or nursing home with a great big smile, and to stop by the table with the Down child and touch his shoulder and tell him and his parents what a wonderful family they are. The truth is—the wonder is that they are beautiful in and of themselves and just as they are if only we have eyes to see. The words of Christ are literally true: "whatever you do unto these, you do for me." And what we do for Christ we do for them and for ourselves and for the whole human race. For all of us, each of us, are one.

The new science of metapsychiatry validates this teaching by demonstrating that we all have a spiritual faculty to enter a rehab room and see the Christ who plays in ten thousand places, to help a homeless woman push her shopping cart across the street and know that the story of St. Christopher is the story of us all. Metapsychiatry calls this ability to realize what is really before our eyes the faculty of Beholding. Beholding is a higher faculty than the intellect or imagination or intuition, but one we have not been taught to cultivate. To behold is to see the invisible (what is real and lasting) in the visible (what appears and disappears). The body comes and goes, but the spirit remains forever. St. Paul teaches: "Look not at the things that which are seen but at the things which are not seen, for the things which are seen are temporal while the things which are not seen are eternal" (2 Corinthians 4: 18). Psychiatrist

Thomas Hora (1914–1995), who founded metapsychiatry upon the teachings of Jesus and spiritual learnings from other religions as well as psychiatry, writes:

> There is more to man than meets the eye. We all have the faculty to discern spiritual qualities in the world. We can see honesty; we can see integrity; we can see beauty; we can see love; we can see goodness; we can see joy; we can see peace; we can see harmony; we can see intelligence; and so forth. None of these things has any form; none of these things can be imagined; none of these things is tangible, and yet they can be seen. What is the organ that sees these invisible things? Some people call it the soul, spirit, or consciousness. Man is a spiritual being endowed with spiritual faculties of perception.

Each of us can behold the truth of being in all of us.

Prayer

Jesus, the next time I see someone with what doctors call cerebral palsy or Down Syndrome, grace me with the sight to appreciate her just as she is and to realize what is really there: goodness, innocence, love, joy, intelligence, and abundant beauty. You embraced lepers and felt purity and the scales fell from their faces. Help me to know, right now: when I look at anyone I am looking at my Self, I am looking at You, for all of us, each of us, is a spiritual aspect of You and only You! God bless everyone! I close my eyes now and remember someone I've passed by or ignored and ask You to see Love for me. I am learning that I can behold You and everyone with the same eyes that You behold us. I am going to sit still now and listen . . . and see . . .

Thank you, Jesus. I have to go now and call someone up or maybe go to the hospital.

Love Notes

I see Jesus in every human being. I say to myself, this is hungry Jesus, I must feed him. This is sick Jesus. This one has leprosy or gangrene; I must wash him and tend to him. I serve because I love Jesus.

—MOTHER TERESA

Just as the body is one but has many members, and all the members of the body, being many, are one body, so also is the body of Christ.

—I CORINTHIANS 12:12

So if one part of the body suffers, every part suffers with it. If one part is honored, every part rejoices with it.

—I CORINTHIANS 12:26

The Way of Love

*We are one, after all, you and I, togeth-
er we suffer, together exist and forever
will recreate one another.*

—Pierre Teilhard de Chardin

*Everyone is your brother and sister.
Including the flowers, the trees, the animals, the bedbugs, the cockroaches, the
mountains, the sky, the sick people, the
healthy people, the poor people, the rich
people. When you can look at everyone
with one I and not differentiate. Then
you're in love.*

—Robert Adams

64

Christ in the Subway

Caryll Houselander

I was in an underground train, a crowded train in which all sorts of people jostled together, sitting and strap-hanging workers of every description going home at the end of the day. Quite suddenly I saw with my mind, but as vividly as a wonderful picture, Christ in them all. But I saw more than that; not only was Christ in every one of them, living in them, dying in them, rejoicing in them, sorrowing in them—but because He was in them, and because they were here, the whole world was here too, here in this underground train; not only the world as it was at that moment, not only all the people in all the countries of the world, but all those people who had lived in the past and all those yet to come.

I came out into the street and walked for a long time in crowds. It was the same here, on every side, in every passerby, everywhere—Christ. . . .

The "vision" lasted with that intensity for several days. . . . It altered the course of my life completely.

Christ is everywhere; in Him every kind of life has a meaning and has an influence on every other kind of life. It is not the foolish sinner like myself, running about the world with reprobates and feeling magnanimous, who comes closest to them and brings them healing; it is the contemplative in her cell who has never set eyes on them, but in whom Christ fasts and prays for them—or it may be a charwoman in whom Christ makes Himself a servant again, or a king whose crown of gold hides a crown of thorns. Realization of our oneness in Christ is the only cure for human loneliness. For me, too, it is the only ultimate meaning of life, the only thing that gives meaning and purpose to every life.

God's Disguise

Mother Teresa

If sometimes our poor people have had to die of starvation it is not because God didn't care for them, but because you and I didn't give, were not instruments of love in the hands of God, to give them that bread, to give them that clothing; because we did not recognize him, when once more Christ came in distressing disguise—in the hungry man, in the lonely man, in the homeless child, and seeking for shelter.

God has identified himself with the hungry, the sick, the naked, the homeless; hunger, not only for bread, but for love, for care, to be somebody to someone; nakedness, not of clothing only, but nakedness of that compassion that very few people give to the unknown; homelessness, not only just for a shelter made of stone, but that homelessness that comes from having no one to call your own.

Remember,
There Is the Face of Christ

Óscar Romero

Each time we look upon the poor, on the farm workers
who harvest the coffee, the sugarcane, or the cotton or the
farmer who joins the caravan of workers looking to earn
their savings for the year . . . remember, there is the face
of Christ. . . . The face of Christ is among the sacks and
baskets of the farmworkers; the face of Christ is among
those who are tortured and mistreated in the prisons; the
face of Christ is dying of hunger in the children who
have nothing to eat; the face of Christ is in the poor who
ask the church for their voice to be heard. How can the
church deny this request when it is Christ who is telling
us to speak for him?

Christ in the Poor

Jim Forest

Christ identifies himself with those in the most urgent conditions of need: the hungry, thirsty, naked, homeless, sick, and imprisoned. The lesson is simple. In responding to the desperate needs of others, we respond to him: "As you did to the last person, you did to me."

Dorothy Day often said, "Those who cannot see Christ in the poor are atheists indeed."

It is not only in words that Christ identified with those who have nothing and are regarded with contempt. He was born in a stable because no better place was offered for his mother to give birth. As a child he was a refugee. He was imprisoned and died a criminal's death. Given all that, is it a surprise that God's hospitality to us is linked to our hospitality to those who have little or nothing? If we avoid Christ in the poor, we are avoiding the gate to heaven.

We're All God's Children

Dennis Moorman

Soon after moving into my two-room, mud-brick house in the village of Pièla in Burkina Faso where I was serving as a Peace Corps volunteer, I realized that I had moved into the section of town where many of the women who worked as prostitutes were also living. They were mostly foreigners like me. Despite this fact, a lot of neighborhood kids would often come and visit me.

One day I started to play Frisbee with a young boy who had stopped by for a visit. While we were playing, one of the young women who worked in a bar as a prostitute started watching us. After a little while, I threw the Frisbee to her, and she joined in with our fun. Then a little while later, an old man came walking by and started watching us play. Pretty soon the young woman threw the Frisbee to him. He dropped the Frisbee and his cane too, but then clumsily picked it back up and threw it to the young boy.

And there we were, the most unlikely mix of people in a little African village: an old man, a prostitute, a little boy, and a foreigner, all standing together in a circle, throwing a Frisbee, and having fun together. When I reflected on this experience later, I realized that I had received a vision of what the reign of God is all about: love, equality, beauty, and enjoyment with no one excluded or left out.

Love Notes

When you meet anyone,
Remember it is a holy encounter.
As you see him you will see yourself.
As you treat him you will treat yourself.
As you think of him you will think
of yourself.
Never forget this, for in him
You will find yourself,
Or lose yourself.

—A COURSE IN MIRACLES

It is at that time you will know that
I am in My Father, and you are in Me,
and I in you.

—JOHN 14:20

If I love myself,
I love you.
If I love you,

Love Notes

I love myself.
I am in you
and I am you.
No one can understand this
until he has lost his mind.

—RUMI

Sources and Acknowledgments

Orbis Books has made every effort to identify the owner of each selection in this book, and to obtain permission from the author, publisher, or agent in question. In the event of inadvertent errors, please notify us.

1. Joseph Whelan, "Fall in Love" (often misattributed to Fr. Pedro Arrupe). From *Finding God in All Things: A Marquette Prayer Book*. Copyright © 2009 by Marquette University. Reprinted by permission of Marquette University Press, Milwaukee, WI.

2. Michael Leach, "Love Is the Love of Being Loving." From *National Catholic Reporter*, March 13, 2012.

3. Thomas Hora, "All Things Work Together for Good to Those Who Love Being Loving." From The PAGL Foundation, www.pagl.org.

4. Harold W. Becker, "Unconditional Love." From *Unconditional Love—An Unlimited Way of Being*. Copyright © 2007 by Harold Becker. Reprinted by permission of White Fire Publishing, Orlando, Florida.

5. Kahlil Gibran, "When Love Beckons, Follow." From *The Prophet* by Kahlil Gibran, originally published in 1923 by Alfred A. Knopf.

6. Marianne Williamson, "The Intuitive Knowledge of the Heart." From *A Return to Love* by Marianne Williamson. Copyright © 1992 by Marianne Williamson. Portions reprinted from *A Course in Miracles*. Copyright © 1975 by Foundation for Inner Peace, Inc. Used by permission of HarperCollins Publishers.

7. Anne Lamott, "We Are Love with Skin On." From Anne Lamott's Facebook page. Copyright © 2021 Anne Lamott. Used by permission of The Wylie Agency LLC.

8. Unknown, "I Know Who She Is." Retrieved from various websites on the internet.

9. "The Gift of Love." 1 Corinthians 13:1–13. Scripture quotation taken from the (NASB®) New American Standard Bible®. Copyright © 2020 by The Lockman Foundation. Used by permission. All rights reserved, www.lockman.org.

10. Anthony De Mello, "The Qualities of Love." From *The Way to Love: The Last Meditations of Anthony De Mello* by Anthony De Mello. Copyright © 1991 by Gujarat Sahitya Prakash, Anand, India. Used by permission of Doubleday, an imprint of the Knopf Doubleday Publishing Group, a division of Penguin Random House LLC. All rights reserved.

11. Stephen Colbert, "You Will Truly Serve Only What You Love." From a Commencement address at Northwestern University, June 17, 2011.

12. Philip Walsh, "Justice Is What Love Looks Like In Public." From Maine Initiatives website, https://maineinitiatives.org/stay-in-the-know/justice-is-what-love-looks-like-in-public. Used by permission of Philip Walsh.

13. Mother Teresa, "Love and the Purpose of Life." From excellencereporter.com, February 21, 2019.

14. Ilia Delio, "The Daring Adventure of Love." From *Franciscan Prayer.* Copyright © 2004 by Ilia Delio. Published by St. Anthony Messenger Press.

15. Carlo Carretto, "Love Is for Living." From *Love Is for Living* by Carlo Carretto. English Translation, Copyright © 1976 by Darton, Longman and Todd Ltd. and Orbis Books.

16. Jack Kornfield, "Love Is Mysterious." From *A Path with Heart: A Guide Through the Perils and Promises of Spiritual Life* by Jack Kornfield. Copyright © 1993 by Jack Kornfield. Used by permission of Bantam Books, an imprint of Random House, a division of Penguin Random House LLC. All rights reserved.

17. Thomas Merton, "Love Sails Me Around the House." From *The Sign of Jonas* by Thomas Merton. Copyright 1953 by the Abbey of Our Lady of Gethsemani; copyright renewed 1981 by The Trustees of the Merton Legacy Trust. Published by Houghton Mifflin Harcourt Publishing Company.

18. Matthew Fox, "What Is This Thing Called Love?" Original essay written for *The Way of Love*. Copyright © 2022 by Matthew Fox.

19. Eckhart Tolle, "This Is Love." From *The Power of Now: A Guide to Spiritual Enlightenment*. Copyright © 1999 by Eckhart Tolle. Used by permission of Namaste Publishing.

Meister Eckhart, "Become Love." From *Meister Eckhart's Book of Secrets* by Mark S. Burrows and Jon M. Sweeney. Copyright © 2019. Used by permission of Hampton Roads Publishing c/o Red Wheel/Weiser, LLC Newburyport, MA, www.redwheelweiser.com.

Sheri Bessi-Eckert, "Be That One." From thewellnessuniverse. com blog.

20. Bishop Michael Curry, "The Power of Love (or Imagine a World Where Love Is the Way)." From *The Power of Love: Sermons, Reflections, and Wisdom to Uplift and Inspire* by Bishop Michael Curry. Copyright © 2018 by Bishop Michael Curry. Used by permission of Avery, an imprint of Penguin Publishing Group, a division of Penguin Random House LLC. All rights reserved.

21. Donna Goddard, "May We Remember that God Is the Only Love." Gratitude Prayer from *Strange Words: Poems and Prayers*. Copyright © 2020 by Donna Goddard. Used by permission of Donna Goddard.

22. St. Augustine, "What Do I Love When I Love God." From *The Confessions of St. Augustine.*

23. Ernesto Cardenal, "God's Signature." From *Abide in Love*. Copyright © 1995 by Orbis Books.

24. Richard Rohr, "Start With Loving a Stone." From *What the Mystics Know*. Copyright 2019 © by Richard Rohr. Reprinted by arrangement with The Crossroad Publishing Company, www.crossroadpublishing.com.

25. Patrick T. Reardon, "God Is the Ocean in Which We All Swim." From *National Catholic Reporter,* Soul Seeing, September 18, 2018. Reprinted by permission of Patrick T. Reardon.

26. Søren Kierkegaard. "Our Love Flows from the Love of God." From *Works of Love* originally published in 1847.

27. Robert Ellsberg, "We Love Because He First Loved Us." From "Learning to Love" from *The Saints' Guide to Happiness: Practical Lessons in the Life of the Spirit* by Robert Ellsberg. Copyright © 2003 by Robert Ellsberg. Reprinted by permission of North Point Press, a division of Farrar, Straus and Giroux. All Rights Reserved.

28. A Course in Miracles, "I Am Sustained by the Love of God." From *A Course in Miracles*. Lesson 50, ACIM, W-50.1:1–4:8.

29. Vickie Leach, "God Is a Mother, Too." From the book *Chicken Soup for the Mother & Daughter Soul* by Jack Canfield, Mark Victor Hansen, Dorothy Firman, Julie Firman, and Frances Firman Salorio. Copyright © 2012 by Chicken Soup for the Soul Publishing, LLC. Published by Backlist, LLC, a unit of Chicken Soup for the Soul Publishing, LLC. Chicken Soup for the Soul is a registered trademark of Chicken Soup for the Soul Publishing, LLC. Reprinted by permission. All rights reserved.

30. Thea Bowman, "God Is My Everything." Reprinted by permission of Franciscan Sisters of Perpetual Adoration / fspa. org/theabowman.

31. Madeleine Delbrêl, "Quick, Open the Door, It's God Coming to Love Us!" From *We, the Ordinary People of the Streets*, trans. David Louis Schindler, Jr. and Charles F. Mann. Copyright © 2000 by Wm. B. Eerdmans Publishing Company. Reprinted by permission of the publisher; all rights reserved.

32. Marion Amberg, "I Love You for Sentimental Reasons." From *National Catholic Reporter,* Soul Seeing, June 12, 2018: "God Is Love, and God's Face Was Looking at Me for Two Years." Reprinted by permission of Marion Amberg.

33. Brian Doyle, "God." From *How the Light Gets In*, p. 117. Copyright © 2015 by Brian Doyle. Orbis Books, Maryknoll, NY.

34. Gae Rusk, "God Owns a Convenience Store in British Columbia—Who Knew?" From *A Sense of Wonder,* edited by Brian Doyle. Copyright © 2016 by *Portland Magazine*. Orbis Books, Maryknoll, NY.

Sources and Acknowledgments

35. Luke 10:11–32, "The Parable of the Prodigal Son." From Today's Good News website, https://www.goodnews.ie/prdigalson.shtml.

36. Dom Eugene Boylan, "This Tremendous Lover." From *This Tremendous Lover* by Dom Eugene Boylan. Copyright © 2019 by Mount St. Joseph Abbey of Roscrea. Published by Baronius Press.

37. Josephine Robertson, "Don't Give Up on God, or Yourself." From Josephine Robertson's website www.crazywholelife.com. Reprinted by permission of Rev. Josephine Robertson.

38. Unknown, "That We May Love as You Love!" From the Jesuit Resource website, https://www.xavier.edu/jesuitresource/online-resources/prayer-index/gods-love.

39. Joy Scrivener, "I Am Wherever There Is Love." According to the *San Antonio Express News*, Greg and Joy Scrivener and their three children suffered the loss of Abbey, their 14-year-old dog, in mid-August 2006. This story, attributed to Joy Scrivener, is widely available on the internet under a variety of titles, including "Going Postal," "Angels at the Post Office," "Angels Turn Up In Unexpected Places," and "This is a US Postal Service Story."

40. Luke 10:25–37, "The Parable of the Good Samaritan." From Bread of Life website, Gospel Reading of the Day, https://breadoflifebangalore.com/gospel/luke-1025-37/#.

41. Frederick Buechner, "Who Is My Neighbor?" From *Wishful Thinking: A Seeker's ABC*, pp. 65–66. Copyright © 1973 by Frederick Buechner. Harper and Row.

42. Cynthia Bourgeault, "Love Your Neighbor." From Cynthia Bourgeault, *The Wisdom Jesus: Transforming Heart and Mind—A New Perspective on Christ and His Message*, pp. 31–32. Copyright © 2008 by Cynthia Bourgeault. Reprinted by arrangement with The Permissions Company LLC on behalf of Shambhala Publications Inc., Boulder, Colorado, www.shambhala.com.

43. Matt Kahn. "Love Whatever Arises." From Matt Kahn's writings. Used by permission of Matt Kahn, All for Love, https://mattkahn.org/.

44. Edwina Gateley, "Love from Neighbors on the Margins." From *Christ in the Margins* by Robert Lentz and Edwina Gateley, pp. 109–110. Text copyright © 2003 by Edwina Gateley. Orbis Books, Maryknoll, NY.

45. Mary Rita Schilke Sill, "When You Thought I Wasn't Looking." Copyright © 1980 by Mary Rita Schilke Sill. Reprinted by permission of Mary Rita Schilke Sill.

46. Victor M. Parachin, "Loving-Kindness: Blessing Your Corner of the World with Love." From *Eastern Wisdom for Western Minds,* pp. 84–86. Copyright © 2007 by Victor M. Parachin. Orbis Books, Maryknoll, NY.

47. "Love Your Enemies." Matthew 5:38–45, retrieved from evangeli.net, Sunday 7th (A) in Ordinary Time, https://evangeli.net/gospel/day/IV_61 and Luke 6:27–36, retrieved from evangeli.net, Thursday of the Twenty-third Week in Ordinary Time, https://evangeli.net/gospel/day/IV_211.

48. Ram Dass and Paul Gorman, "We Love Each Other. That's Enough." From *How Can I Help?: Stories and Reflections on Service* by Ram Dass and Paul Gorman. Copyright © 1985 by Ram Dass and Paul Gorman. Used by permission of Alfred A. Knopf, an imprint of the Knopf Doubleday Publishing Group, a division of Penguin Random House LLC. All rights reserved.

49. Donna Ashworth, "Save Your Best for Someone Else." From *The Right Words.* Copyright © 2021 by Donna Ashworth. Reprinted by permission of Donna Ashworth.

50. John Lewis, "Love at Its Best." From On Being with Krista Tippet: "John Lewis—Love in Action." Used by permission of On Being with Krista Tippett, https://onbeing.org/programs/john-lewis-love-in-action/.

51. Vincent P. Cole, "Why Are You Here?" From *What They Taught Us: How Maryknoll Missioners Were Evangelized by the Poor,* edited by Joseph A. Heim, p. 28. Copyright © 2009 by Joseph A. Heim. Orbis Books, Maryknoll, NY.

52. Walt Whitman, "Stand Up for the Stupid and Crazy." From *Leaves of Grass,* 1855.

53. Henri Nouwen, "Love Deeply." From *The Inner Voice of Love: A Journey Through Anguish to Freedom.* Copyright © 1996 by Henri Nouwen. Used by permission of Doubleday, an imprint of the Knopf Doubleday Publishing Group, a division of Penguin Random House LLC. All rights reserved.

54. Joyce Rupp, "A Piece of Light." From *A Cosmic Dance* by Joyce Rupp, p. 85. Text copyright © 2002 by Joyce Rupp. Orbis Books, Maryknoll, NY.

55. Pauline Hovey, "Tend to What Repulses You." From *National Catholic Reporter,* Soul Seeing, March 10, 2020. Reprinted by permission of Pauline Hovey.

56. Brené Brown, "Don't Look Away." Retrieved from the Internet. Used by permission of Brené Brown, research professor, University of Houston.

57. Joseph G. Healey, "Having Lunch with God." From *Once Upon a Time in Africa,* pp. 121–22. Copyright © 2004 by Joseph G. Healey. Orbis Books, Maryknoll, NY.

58. Michael Leach, "Bishop Morrie Says It's Not about the Soup." From *National Catholic Reporter,* Soul Seeing, June 30, 2015.

59. Fran Rossi Szpylczyn, "It All Tastes Like Love." From *National Catholic Reporter,* Soul Seeing, August 28, 2012. Reprinted by permission of Fran Rossi Szpylczyn.

60. Wendell Berry, "A Marriage, an Elegy." From *New Collected Poems.* Copyright © 1973 by Wendell Berry. Reprinted with the permission of The Permissions Company, LLC on behalf of Counterpoint Press, counterpointpress.com. [We found this first in Spirituality & Practice: Resources for Spiritual Journeys, the multifaith and interspiritual website founded by Frederic and Mary Ann Brussat (spiritualityandpractice.com).]

61. Thomas Merton, "Loving the Christ in Others." From "The Power and Meaning of Love," in *Disputed Questions* by Thomas Merton. Copyright © 1960 by The Abbey of Our Lady of Gethsemani. Copyright renewed 1988 by Alan Hanson. Reprinted by permission of Farrar, Straus, & Giroux. All Rights Reserved.

62. David Adam, "Christ, Let Me See You in Others." From *Just One Year,* p. 130. Copyright © 2006 by Timothy Radcliffe.

Darton, Longman, and Todd, London, and Orbis Books, Maryknoll, NY.

63. Michael Leach, "Christ and Cerebral Palsy." From *National Catholic Reporter,* Soul Seeing, November 11, 2011.

64. Caryll Houselander, "Christ in the Subway." From *A Rocking Horse Catholic.* New York: Sheed and Ward, 1955.

65. Mother Teresa, "God's Disguise." From *A Gift for God: Prayers and Meditations*, pp. 24–25. Copyright © 1975 by Mother Teresa Missionaries of Charity. Harper & Row, NY.

66. Oscar Romero, "Remember, There Is the Face of Christ." From *Monseñor Oscar A. Romero: Su pensamiento*, vol. 5, November 26, 1978, homily, 327.

67. Jim Forest, "Christ in the Poor." From *Confession: Doorway to Forgiveness*, pp. 109–110. Copyright © 2002 by Jim Forest. Orbis Books, Maryknoll, NY.

68. Dennis Moorman, "We're All God's Children." From *Why Not Be a Missioner? Young Maryknollers Tell Their Stories*, edited by Michael Leach and Susan Perry, p. 97. Copyright © 2002 by Orbis Books, Maryknoll, NY.

Index of Contributors

David Adam (d. 2020) was a British Anglican priest, writer, and much-loved figure in the field of Celtic spirituality............. **62**

Marion Amberg is an award-winning journalist and author of several books, including *Penny Prayers: True Stories of Change* and *Monuments, Marvels, and Miracles: A Traveler's Guide to Catholic America*......... **32**

Donna Ashworth of Scotland is a writer, poet, and the woman behind the popular website Ladies Pass It On. She is author of *The Right Words*, *To the Women*, and *History Will Remember When the World Stopped*.. **49**

Augustine of Hippo, also known as Saint Augustine, was a theologian, philosopher, and the bishop of Hippo Regius in Numidia, Roman North Africa, in the fourth century. His *Confessions* is a spiritual classic.. **22**

Harold W. Becker, a modern-day messenger of unconditional love, founded the nonprofit the Love Foundation and conceived Global Love Day, an annual celebration of humanity............. **4**

Wendell Erdman Berry is an American novelist, poet, essayist, environmental activist, cultural critic, and farmer. He has published more than eighty books, including *The Unsettling of America*, in which he argues that good farming is a cultural development and spiritual discipline. **60**

Sheri Bessi-Eckert, author of the multi-award-winning blog Dear Human—Letters to Humanity, is a professional counselor whose holistic approach includes mindfulness as a means of healing and growth.. **19**

Cynthia Bourgeault is a modern-day mystic, Episcopal priest, prolific author, and faculty member at the Center for Action and Contemplation. She is founding director of an international network of Wisdom Schools... **42**

Thea Bowman (d. 1990) was a Black Catholic religious sister, teacher, and scholar who made a major contribution to the ministry of the Catholic Church toward her fellow African Americans... **30**

Dom Eugene Boylan, OCR (d. 1964) was an Irish-born Trappist monk, priest, and writer. He published two books: *This Tremendous Lover* and *Difficulties in Mental Prayer*....................................... **36**

Brené Brown is an American professor, lecturer, podcast host, and author of many bestselling books, including *The Gifts of Imperfection* and *Dare to Lead*... **56**

Frederick Buechner is an American writer, novelist, poet, autobiographer, essayist, preacher, and theologian. He is an ordained Presbyterian minister and the author of more than thirty books.. **41**

Ernesto Cardenal (d. 2020) was a Nicaraguan Catholic priest, poet, and politician. He was a liberation theologian and the founder of the primitivist art community in the Solentiname Islands, where he lived for more than ten years **23**

Index of Contributors

Carlo Carretto (d. 1988) was an Italian writer, mystic, and member of the Little Brothers of Jesus, who modeled himself upon desert contemplative Charles de Foucauld..................................... **15**

Stephen Colbert is a comedian, writer, producer, political commentator, actor, and television host best known for hosting *The Colbert Report* and *The Late Show with Stephen Colbert*............ **11**

Vincent P. Cole is a Maryknoll missionary priest who was among the first to arrive in Indonesia forty years ago. He is the last working Catholic American priest in Papua, and one of the last three in Indonesia... **51**

Michael Curry is presiding bishop and primate of the Episcopal Church in the USA. He is the chief pastor and serves as president and chief executive officer, and as chair of the Executive Council of the Episcopal Church. **20**

Ram Dass (d. 2019) was an American spiritual teacher, psychologist, and author. His book *Be Here Now* helped popularize Eastern spirituality and yoga in the West... **48**

Madeleine Delbrêl (d. 1964) was a French Catholic author, poet, and mystic, whose works include the posthumous publications *We, the Ordinary People of the Streets* and *The Joy of Believing*.......... **31**

Ilia Delio, OSF, a Franciscan Sister of Washington, DC, holds the Josephine C. Connelly Endowed Chair in Theology at Villanova University and is author of seventeen books, several of which have won awards, including *The Unbearable Wholeness of Being*.. **14**

The Way of Love

Anthony de Mello (d. 1987) was a teacher, author, and spiritual master. His books sell worldwide and help millions of people gain awareness and peace.. **10**

Brian Doyle (d. 2017) was editor of *Portland Magazine* and author of many books of essays and fiction, notably the novels *Mink River* and *The Plover*. He is widely considered the finest Catholic writer of his generation.. **33**

Meister Eckhart (d. 1328) was a German theologian, philosopher, and mystic, born near Gotha in the Landgraviate of Thuringia in the Holy Roman Empire. His work continues to be read and shared today. **19**

Robert Ellsberg, publisher and editor-in-chief of Orbis Books, is author of many award-winning books, including *A Living Gospel, All Saints, Blessed among All Women, The Saints' Guide to Happiness*, and *Blessed among Us*.. **27**

Jim Forest is an American writer, Orthodox Christian lay theologian, educator, and peace activist whose biographies of Thomas Merton, Daniel Berrigan, and Dorothy Day have won wide acclaim..... **67**

Matthew Fox is a spiritual theologian, Episcopal priest, and activist for gender justice and eco-justice. He has written scores of bestselling books and is particularly known for contributions to creation spirituality and his engagement with the Christian mystical tradition...**18**

Edwina Gateley is a poet, theologian, artist, writer, and modern-day mystic and prophet. Her many books include *Christ in the Margins*, and *Soul Sisters: Women in Scripture Speak to Women Today*....... **44**

206

Index of Contributors

Kahlil Gibran (d. 1931) was a Lebanese American writer, poet, and visual artist whose book *The Prophet* is one of the bestselling books of all time.. **5**

Donna Goddard of Australia shares her love for the Divine and mankind and her understanding of the causes of suffering and happiness. She is author of *The Love of Being Loving* and *The Love of Devotion*. **21**

Paul Gorman, a former radio program producer and talk show host in New York City, is coauthor of *How Can I Help? Stories and Reflections on Service*, with Ram Dass. **48**

Joseph Healey, a Maryknoll missionary priest specializing in small Christian communities (also known as basic ecclesial communities) is a teacher, researcher, and author of several books, including *Once Upon a Time in Africa: Stories of Wisdom and Joy*. **57**

Thomas Hora (d. 1995) was the founder of metapsychiatry, a method of healing that integrates principles from metaphysics, spirituality, and psychology. His books include *Beyond the Dream: Awakening to Reality*. **3**

Caryll Houselander (d. 1954) was a lay Roman Catholic ecclesiastical artist, mystic, popular religious writer, and poet........... **64**

Pauline Hovey is a writer living in southern New Mexico where she accompanies migrants and refugees at a hospitality center in El Paso, Texas. **55**

Matt Kahn is a spiritual teacher, healer, and a popular YouTube speaker. He is the bestselling author of *Whatever Arises, Love That* and *Everything Is Here to Help You*. **43**

Søren Kierkegaard (d. 1855) was a Danish philosopher, theologian, poet, social critic, and religious author who is widely considered to be the first existentialist philosopher. **26**

Jack Kornfield is an American author and teacher in the Vipassana movement in American Theravada Buddhism. Trained as a Buddhist monk in Thailand, Burma, and India, he is one of the key teachers to introduce Buddhist mindfulness practices to the West. **16**

Anne Lamott is an American writer, political activist, and public speaker. Her books include the bestselling *Traveling Mercies* and *Hallelujah Anyway: Rediscovering Mercy*. **7**

Michael Leach, publisher emeritus of Orbis Books, has edited and published more than three thousand books over a fifty-year career, still in progress. He is grateful to be married to his best friend, Vickie, also for more than fifty years. **2, 58, 63**

Vickie Leach, wife, mother, and educator, was assistant principal at Stamford High School and has enjoyed having it all. She is grateful to be married to her best friend, Michael, for more than fifty years. **29**

John Lewis (d. 2021), an American statesman and civil rights leader, was the US Representative for Georgia's 5th Congressional District. **48**

Thomas Merton (d. 1968) was one of the most prolific and influential spiritual writers of the twentieth century. A monk, poet, and social activist, Merton wrote numerous books, including his monumental autobiography, *The Seven Storey Mountain*. **17, 61**

Index of Contributors

Dennis Moorman, a Maryknoll missionary priest, is currently based in São Paulo, Brazil. He travels worldwide helping trauma victims heal... **68**

Henri Nouwen (d. 1996) was a Dutch Catholic priest and one of the most popular spiritual writers of the twentieth century. He was author of more than forty books, including *The Wounded Healer* and *Adam: God's Beloved*... **53**

Victor Parachin is an ordained minister in the Christian Church (Disciples of Christ) and the author of *Lessons in Living from the 23rd Psalm* and *Eastern Wisdom for Western Minds*.................... **46**

Patrick T. Reardon is a writer, essayist, poet, and expert on the history of Chicago. Author of ten books, including *Requiem for David*, a poetry collection about his brother's suicide, he also enjoyed a successful career as a leading reporter for the *Chicago Tribune* **25**

Josephine Robertson, an ordained Episcopal priest who leads a congregation in Bellevue Washington, has a Master of Divinity and has spent nearly twenty-five years as a true spiritual geek. **37**

Richard Rohr, OFM, Franciscan priest and founder of the Center for Action and Contemplation, is a globally recognized ecumenical teacher and author of numerous books on faith, spirituality, and mysticism, including *The Universal Christ*. **24**

St. Óscar Romero (d. 1980), a Salvadoran Roman Catholic archbishop who was a vocal critic of the violent activities of government armed forces, right-wing groups, and leftist guerrillas in El Salvador, was assassinated while saying Mass..................... **66**

Joyce Rupp, a Servite sister, has authored numerous bestselling books on spiritual growth, including *Return to the Root: Reflections on the Inner Life*. She currently serves as director of the Boundless Compassion program. **54**

Gae Rusk, is a writer and a resident of Kaua'i, Hawaii. She is author of *Monsoon Madness*. **34**

Joy Scrivener is a San Antonia mother of three, including Meredith, whose letter to God following the death of her dog Abbey went viral in 2006. .... **39**

Mary Rita Schilke Sill is a language arts teacher and poet. Her most recent poem, "Friends Are Like the Sun," was included in *The Blessings of Friendship* by Mary Engelbreit. **45**

Fran Rossi Szpylczyn is a writer, blogger and social networker. You can explore her work by visiting her blog, There Will Be Bread (blog.timesunion.com/bread). **59**

Mother Teresa (d. 1997) was a Catholic nun who dedicated her life to caring for the destitute and dying in the slums of Calcutta. In 1979 she received the Nobel Peace Prize, and after her death was canonized as Saint Teresa. **13, 65**

Eckhart Tolle is a German spiritual teacher and self-help author best known as the author of *The Power of Now* and *A New Earth: Awakening to Your Life's Purpose*. **19**

Philip Walsh is the executive director of Maine Initiatives, a public, community-based foundation advancing social, economic, and environmental justice in Maine through informed, intentional and collective philanthropy. **60**

Index of Contributors

Joseph P. Whelan (d. 1994), was former provincial superior of the Maryland Province of the Society of Jesus, assistant to the superior general of the Jesuits in Rome and research fellow at the Woodstock Theological Center at Georgetown University. **1**

Walt Whitman (d. 1892) was an American poet, essayist, and journalist. A humanist, he was a part of the transition between transcendentalism and realism, incorporating both views in his works.. **52**

Marianne Williamson is an American author, spiritual leader, politician, and activist. She has written thirteen books, including the mega-bestseller *A Return to Love*. **6**

Someday, after mastering the winds,
the waves, the tides and gravity,
we shall harness for God the energies
of love,
and then, for a second time in the his-
tory of the world,
man will have discovered fire.

—Pierre Teilhard de Chardin